CW00406044

WS 2075011 0

RETURN TO REASON:
POPPER'S THOUGHT IN PUBLIC LIFE

STANDARD LOAN

UNLESS RECALLED BY ANOTHER READER
THIS ITEM MAY BE BORROWED FOR

FOUR WEEKS

To renew, telephone:
01243 816089 (Bishop Otter)
01243 812099 (Bognor Regis)

- 3 MAY 2008

LIBREX —

By the same author

Understanding Medicine (Penguin)

WEST SUSSEX
HIGHER EDUCATION LIBRARY

AUTHOR	ACCESSION No
JAMES, R.	BR20321
TITLE	CLASS No
RETURN TO REASON	192/PoP

RETURN TO REASON

Popper's Thought in Public Life

Roger James

W. SUSSEX INSTITUTE OF
WITHDRAWN

Open Books

First published 1980 by Open Books Publishing Ltd
West Compton House, near Shepton Mallet, Somerset,
England.

© Roger James 1980

Hardback ISBN 0 7291 0163 0
Paperback ISBN 0 7291 0168 1

This title is available in both paperback and hardback
editions. The paperback edition is sold subject to the
condition that it shall not, by way of trade or otherwise,
be lent, resold, hired out or otherwise circulated in
any form of binding or cover other than that in which
it is published and without a similar condition, including
this condition, being imposed on the subsequent purchaser.

All rights reserved. No part of this publication
may be reproduced or transmitted in any form or by
any means, electronic or mechanical, including
photocopy, recording, or any information storage and
retrieval system, without permission in writing from
Open Books Publishing Ltd

Printed in Great Britain by A. Wheaton & Co. Ltd., Exeter

Contents

Introduction   1

1 The importance of criticism   10
2 Three worlds   24
3 Forms of unreason   41
4 Democracy in theory   52
5 Psychology against culture   69
6 Conditioning is an illusion   85
7 The straitjacket of planning   94
8 The concrete Jerusalem   105
9 Blinding with science   128
10 'Some one had blunder'd'   146
11 Democracy in practice   158
12 The power of wrong ideas   177

Bibliography   183

Index   186

Acknowledgements

I want to thank Frank Guy, Allan Low, Geoffrey Broadbent, and Tyrrell Burgess for suggestions and criticisms, Sheila Alexander for typing the first draught, Barbara Broadbent for reading the proofs, Patrick Taylor for making it possible for the book to be published, and last but certainly not least my wife Margaret for constant encouragement.

The substance of chapter six appeared first as an article 'Is conditioning a myth?' in *Higher Education Review* in 1976 and in a revised form under the more confident title 'Conditioning is a myth' in *World Medicine* in 1977. I thank the respective editors for permission to reproduce; and I also thank Sir Karl Popper for permission to reproduce the diagrams from his book *The Logic of Scientific Discovery* which appear on page 87.

Roger James
9 Eastern Villas Road
Portsmouth
December 1979

References to Popper's Works

References in the text to the major works of Sir Karl Popper are given by the initial letters, as below, followed by the page number:

L.Sc.D. (1959) *The Logic of Scientific Discovery* (London: Hutchinson) (first published in 1935 in German as *Logik der Forschung*)

O.S.i and ii (1962) *The Open Society and Its Enemies*, 4th edition revised (London: Routledge and Kegan Paul)

P.H. (1963) *The Poverty of Historicism*, 2nd edition revised (London: Routledge and Kegan Paul)

C.R. (1969) *Conjectures and Refutations*, 3rd edition revised (London: Routledge and Kegan Paul)

O.K. (1972) *Objective Knowledge: An Evolutionary Approach* (Oxford: The Clarendon Press)

U.Q. (1976) *Unended Quest: An Intellectual Autobiography* (London: Fontana/Collins)

S.B. (1977) *The Self and Its Brain* (with J. C. Eccles) (London, Berlin, New York: Springer International)

There is also a quotation from a paper entitled 'The myth of the framework' in *The Abdication of Philosophy: Essays in honor of P. A. Schilpp* (1976) (La Salle, Illinois: Open Court) and from a paper 'The logic of the social sciences' in *The Positivist Dispute in German Sociology* (1976) (London: Heinemann)

Introduction

This book is about departures from reason in the conduct of public affairs and the power of certain wrong ideas and unquestioned assumptions. In exploring this power I shall draw extensively on the philosophy of Sir Karl Popper and I shall show how the disregard of it has led to so much that has gone wrong in our time. Also, very tentatively, I suggest how ways out of some of our troubles might follow from attention to rational methods and Popper's neglected ideas.

Since the second world war, if not before, an unacceptable number of mistakes has been made in the government of this country – and in public life generally – which can be ascribed to mistaken theories held by our leaders, not just politicians and civil servants, but also, perhaps even more, our intellectual and professional leaders. Collectively the mistakes have contributed to, if they have not always been the cause of, our relative economic decline and the decline in national morale and self-confidence. Government policies fail to accomplish their objects and even achieve the opposite (e.g. aim to lessen the gap between rich and poor, yet end up by increasing it) and yet are not publicly acknowledged as failures; large-scale schemes of replanning and reorganization are carried out without any clear object in view and without any published assessment of their necessity or, in retrospect, of their success or failure; extensive powers are given to government agencies by nationalisation or otherwise and then not used in the interest of the public (e.g. the Bank of England's failure to control the fringe banks, indeed its encouragement of them); the physical and economic balance of our cities is destroyed possibly for ever in the name of half-baked theories of planning; and much that is done costs enormously more than it should. (Hospital building is an example. Leslie Chapman quotes the Ministry's former chief architect to the effect that this has cost nearly twice what was necessary − a waste of about £1,500 million in the ten years from 1967 − approaching the lowest estimate of the whole Concorde project.) I give a list of some of the failures I am talking about on pages 40–41. None of these schemes was a response to popular demand, as was, I think it would be true to say, the original setting up of the National Health Service, for example. Some were not even debated in Parliament, and one, the rebuilding of our cities with concrete flats, was done in defiance of the known wishes of the great majority who want a house with a bit of garden. So a central problem of our time comes down to this: how can government be controlled by the governed?

And there has been the blind following of short-sighted expert, especially short-sighted economic, advice. This was typified by the conversion to oil of nearly every coal-burning furnace in the country (when we had no oil of our own) just in time to make us vulnerable when OPEC began to tighten the screws.

Peter Wilmott, writing in an issue of *New Society* devoted to a history of 'brief ideas' − 'The gods that failed' − said: 'What was wrong was not that the assumptions were false or that political pressures distorted the original motion, but just that the policy turned out in application less successful than had been hoped. What often happened was that the particular innovation had secondary consequences which had not been envisaged. The implications had, in fact, not been thought through.' Actually I shall show that some of the assumptions were false; but, more important than that, the instigators of these policies *should have known* that there would be unexpected secondary consequences. It should have been part of their education to expect and guard against them. You cannot even be sure, for example, that a simple soak-the-rich tax will in fact make the rich poorer, still less that it will make the poor richer. The rich may discover new sources of wealth or new tax dodges. The 1964–70 Labour government can hardly be accused of trying to widen the gap between rich and poor. Nevertheless that was the overall result of their administration. And it seems to have been true also of the 1974–9 government.

Most of these brief ideas came into vogue after the publication in 1945 of *The Open Society and its Enemies* in which Popper showed that the main task of the social sciences, if not the only one, was to analyse and as far as possible foresee just these 'secondary consequences' of social and political action. It should not have needed more than a decade of disaster to demonstrate this conclusion.

My thesis is that most of these failures can be attributed to a small number of what can be called philosophical mistakes. They are:

1 Jumping to a solution before clearly formulating what the problem is (or indeed if there is one at all) or how success or failure are to be judged. Achievement of the solution then becomes the goal; and, when opposition develops, the problem becomes how to get the solution accepted, while the question of how best to solve the original problem, if there was one, never gets discussed at all. I call this mistake *solutioneering*.

Robert Heller has brilliantly encapsulated the spirit of this approach as: 'Think of a project; estimate (or, rather, underestimate) its cost; estimate (or, rather, overestimate) the revenue it will generate; and, if an inconvenient gap still exists, close it by valuing the social benefit at the sum required.' Some people's attitude to medicine is the same. The moment you feel unwell you must take some tablets – any tablets, anybody's tablets – regardless of what is wrong with you, of whether it is likely to get better anyway, and of what the tablets are supposed to do.

2 Ignoring the fact that every scheme or reform will have its snags. Some can be foreseen and others cannot; but both the foreseen and the unforeseen must be looked for systematically and corrected.

This is the mistake pointed out by Wilmott above, and by Popper more than thirty years before. I call it by the medical term *tunnel-vision*: keeping your eye so fixed on the rich whom you are squeezing till the pips squeak that you do not notice that the people you are squeezing most are the poor. False economies are examples of this error.

3 *Trendism:* confusing laws with trends.

You can reasonably expect that the deeper you go down into the sea the greater will be the pressure. This depends on the natural *law* of gravitation. You cannot, in the same way, assume that because deaths from tuberculosis declined rapidly from 1950 to 1960 that this unmistakable trend would continue indefinitely. If it had done there would by 1970 have been a negative number of deaths. There would that year have been about 250 cases of resurrection from the dead!

4 The failure to realize that a theory cannot be confirmed merely by finding facts that support it.

Only when a determined search for facts that are incompatible with it has failed, can it be considered corroborated, and even then it remains provisional, a theory and not a fact. I call this very common failure by the term *white-swanning* for reasons that will become apparent in Chapter 1. It is a form of tunnel-vision and, like it, is connected with the invalid process of reasoning known as induction (see Chapter 1); and it leads to mistake number 5.

5 Failure to distinguish between established scientific theories, which have stood up to challenge, and unsubstantiated speculations.

To some extent policy has been based on the uncritical acceptance of theories which are partly dead but will not lie down. Such are the two forms of mutually contradictory deterministic psychology – behaviourism and dynamic or analytic psychology, 'psychologism' (the belief described in Chapter 5 that human behaviour can be explained entirely in terms of human psychology), 'holism' and 'historicism' (Chapter 3), the false antithesis of individualism versus altruism, and, perhaps worst of all, the sociology of knowledge – the idea that truth and knowledge are relative to historical period or social class (Chapter 3).

I am not saying that the planners who planned the new housing estates, or the architects who enthused over their slabs and tower blocks, held consciously the theory that individualism is opposed to concern for others. But this theory and the others I have mentioned formed part of the atmosphere in which they designed their communal landscaped areas on which ball games were prohibited, while the fact that these were discredited theories did *not* form part of that atmosphere. The effect on the ground, as it were, is not necessarily what was meant by the originator of a theory, but is a residual, confused, second-hand, popular version of it.

The point is made very effectively by Dr J. M. Roberts in his brilliant history of the world:

> The message men took from Freud suggested that the unconscious was the true source of most significant behaviour, that moral values and attitudes were projections of the influences which had moulded this unconscious, that, therefore, the idea of responsibility was at best a myth and probably a dangerous one, and that perhaps rationality itself was an illusion. It did not matter much that Freud's own assertions would have been nonsense had this been true, or that this left out the subtlety and science of his work. This was what many people believed he had proved – and still believe. Such a bundle of ideas called in question the very foundation of liberal civilization itself, the idea of the rational,

responsible, consciously-motivated individual, and this was its general importance.

*   *   *

I remember vividly the pleasurable excitement with which, about fifteen years ago, I read the first chapter of Popper's *The Open Society*. I felt an exhilarating breath of fresh air and common sense blowing away the verbiage and the imprecision of works on politics that had previously come my way. I was impressed at once by the lucidity, the punch, and the lack of an unnecessary word, and yet the marvellous readability of this great book written in the early 1940s in English, although English was not his native language. Far away from the conflict as he then was in New Zealand, he regarded *The Open Society* and its shorter companion volume, *The Poverty of Historicism*, as his war effort.

He expected that freedom would again become a central problem under the renewed influence of Marxism and large-scale planning. 'These books were meant', he has recently said, 'as a defence of freedom against totalitarian and authoritarian ideas, and as a warning against the dangers of historicist superstitions.' They grew out of the theory of knowledge that he had developed in his earlier book on the philosophy of science (L.Sc.D) and out of his conviction that 'our often unconscious views on the theory of knowledge and its central problems ("What can we know?", "How certain is our knowledge?") are decisive for our attitude towards ourselves and towards politics' (U.Q. 115).

The remaining twenty-four chapters of *The Open Society* did not let me down. Since then I have read all Popper's books in English. Early in my reading I became convinced that everybody who pontificates about politics and public affairs should digest Popper's arguments and ideas and test his own against them. His philosophy is rational, and therefore extols the importance of clarity of language, of discussion and criticism, of individual human knowledge, and the attitude of reasonableness. At the same time he relentlessly exposes the unreason in so much of modern thought.

In spite of the massive achievement of *The Open Society* and the decisive contributions to the theory of knowledge and the philosophy of science contained in his other published works, Popper is well known only among the initiated. His name is not a household word; and other philosophers have, on the whole, tended to ignore him. One of the reasons for this is, I think, the fact that his writing is so packed with information, and above all with arguments, and so completely lacks padding and irrelevancies that it defies summary. Another reason is the fact that his philosophy has to a large extent developed out of his knowledge of mathematics and physics, which many philosophers (especially those of the Oxford school) do not understand. His scientific understanding enabled him to develop an unprecedented unity of outlook in regard to both science and politics. It enabled him to show, as we shall see, that there is a fundamental similarity and connection between science and democracy. Above all his writing bears the impression of a massive common sense (as well as immense erudition). Although he often points out that the popular view of a problem is mistaken, his conclusions never do violence to common sense. They are never incredible. 'It is important', he wrote, 'to remain in touch with reality, with practice. For those who overlook it have to pay by lapsing into scholasticism' (O.S., ii, 222).

My purpose here is to show the relevance of certain commonly held theories and assumptions, whether explicit or implicit, to what has gone wrong. For detailed arguments and, where appropriate, proofs against those that are ill-founded, the reader is referred to Popper's own works, which he will find lucid and readable. He will also find that the obvious objections that occur to him have also occurred to Popper, and account has been taken of them. These errors that I am concerned with have been perpetrated repeatedly, deliberately, almost cussedly, by leaders of thought and action who have shown a want of the appropriate knowledge that can only be, as Oscar Wilde said in another context, the result of years of study.

In many cases it is in fact the result of three years of study of philosophy at either Oxford or Cambridge. (In support of this comment I point to an article by L. Jonathan Cohen (1978), an Oxford philosopher, which demonstrates his failure to grasp the matter of great practical importance which is the subject of my first chapter; and I quote the remark by Richard Dawkins, an Oxford biologist whose important work I draw on later in this book, that 'philosophy and the subjects known as "humanities" are still taught almost as though Darwin had never lived'.)

Although there are of course other rationalist philosophers and other philosophers whose work has practical applications, I think it is fair to say that in these respects of rationality and relevance Popper stands head and shoulders above the rest. Those practical items of his philosophy that I have been particularly concerned with have been publicly available for up to thirty years and have withstood a good deal of criticism. He carefully explained in advance the very mistakes that were then duly made on our behalf. Against this our top people (with honourable exceptions) have bumbled on, not allowing it to be known just what stars they are following.

As Popper himself freely admitted, the decision (which I shall go into more fully in Chapter 3) to adopt a rational attitude cannot itself be justified by reason. It is more of a moral decision and is justified only by looking at the consequences of irrationalism, that is of allowing the head to be over-ruled by the heart, but not only by the heart. The particular antithesis that I shall stress is not so much between intellect and emotion as between, on the one hand, intelligent foresight aided by criticism and discussion, and on the other, automatic, unthinking reaction and doing only what has always been done before. Emotion, I suspect, can be a useful check on rational action. If doing what seems rational is accompanied by unpleasant emotion, I take it as being an indication that the rational assessment has left important factors out of account. Emotion I see as a kind of feed-back that monitors action and takes in wider aspects of the case than can be held in conscious attention.

In this country, especially, we are apt to neglect philosophy. We mostly feel no need for any *Weltanschaung* or coherent world view. We tend to carry on with an assortment of maxims gleaned from diverse sources, from Shakespeare to Marx, from what father always used to say to what the television pundits tell us, and not to look too closely at the hidden assumptions we are making. The scrutiny of these largely unconscious private 'philosophies' that we all have is, Popper thinks, the main task and the main justification for the existence of formal philosophy.

Before the invention of glass, it was not possible for a house in winter to have both adequate warmth and adequate daylight. The possible variations between on the one hand, large window spaces letting in light and cold, and, on the other warmth with no windows and no light, can be thought of as lying in one line; while the solution, the fitting of glass into moderate window spaces, did not lie at any point on the line but, as it were, at right angles to it. The solution was neither extremist – no heat or no light – nor a compromise, nor revolutionary in the sense of scrapping everything and starting afresh. What was necessary was an entirely new invention superimposed on otherwise adequate houses. Human reason is, in evolutionary terms, an entirely new invention which can be superimposed on our automatic responses.

The earlier chapters in what follows are devoted mostly to theory, to an exposition of those aspects of Popper's philosophy whose neglect has led to what has gone wrong. The later chapters deal with a selection of blunders in our recent history, interpreted in the light of theory, which might have been averted had our experts been better educated.

1

The importance of criticism

'The central mistake is . . . the quest for certainty.'
Popper: O.K.63

Although by no means everybody makes a study of philosophy in the way that we all study arithmetic, everybody has what may be called his own philosophy, picked up in much the same way as he picks up his native language. But whereas his language is out in the open and subject to correction, and other people's language is out in the open and available as good or bad example, philosophies tend to be private and seldom made explicit. This fact, Popper believes, is the main justification for the study of philosophy – because our private, almost unconscious, philosophies are, unless they have been clearly expressed and revised, usually full of errors and mistaken assumptions.

Popper cites a very common mistaken philosophical assumption which he calls the conspiracy theory. This is the assumption that bad things like wars, slumps, unemployment, rising prices etc., are the result of well laid plans by those who stand to gain privately by the public discomfort – armaments manufacturers, employers of cheap labour, profiteers of all kinds. In fact this is not true. Nearly all those bad things are the unintended consequences of the actions of individuals or firms or governments with quite other intentions. When you negotiate to buy a house, the last thing you intend is to put up the price of houses in that district. Nevertheless your action has that tendency; and if a number of people enter the market and bid for the same house, a rise of price is certainly the result. The enormous rise in property prices in the early 1970s was not the result of a sinister plot by those who owned property, but the unforeseen consequence of well-intentioned, if naive, attempts to enable more people to own their houses by, amongst other things, making available 100 per cent mortgages, without increasing the supply of houses. (We are now preparing to do it again – for 'First-time buyers'.) Similarly the high unemployment together with high inflation which we are now experiencing (an impossible combination in a laissez-faire economy) is the result of 'good' attemps to prevent a wage explosion while at the same time providing unemployment – and supplementary – benefits at a level which discourages work for very low wages. Efforts to improve the productivity of industry, to increase the output per man, were not undertaken with the object of creating unemployment, yet unemployment has certainly been one consequence. What *looks* like conspiracy is more often what I have called tunnel-vision or mere muddle. 'I do not wish to imply', Popper writes

> that conspiracies never happen. On the contrary, they are typical social phenomena. They become important, for example, whenever people who believe in the conspiracy theory get into power. And people who sincerely believe that they know how to make heaven on earth are most likely to adopt the conspiracy theory, and to get involved in a counter-conspiracy against non-existing conspirators. For the only explanation of their failure to produce their heaven is the evil intention of the Devil, who has a vested interest in hell.
>
> Conspiracies occur, it must be admitted. But the striking fact which, in spite of their occurrence, disproves the conspiracy theory is that few of these conspiracies are ultimately successful. (O.S., ii, 95)

This is not to deny that there are occasional successful conspiracies. According to Mick Hamer (*Wheels within Wheels*) the strategic motorway network was such a one. But they are not often successful, certainly not more often than the overt plans of individuals and governments. They are therefore not very important in their consequences –

nothing like so important as the unintended consequences of well-meant or rational actions. The analysis and, where possible, the foreseeing of these unintended 'side-effects' is, Popper believes, the main task of the social sciences, not long-range prophecy. (It is only fair to say that Marx was probably the first to state this sort of view; but for a full discussion of this I refer the reader to *The Open Society*, ii, p. 323, note 11 to Chapter 14.)

The fallacy of the conspiracy theory is the first among several of Popper's philosophical conclusions which have consequences for the way we think about our private lives and public affairs, and which differ, in some cases rather strikingly, from the philosophical assumptions which underlie what we read in the press, see on television, and hear from public figures both in government and education.

A second fallacy is a particularly pernicious one: 'A man's opinions are always determined by his economic or political interests'. This, Popper says, becomes 'If you do not hold the same views as I, you must be dominated by some sinister economic (or political) motives' (Magee, 1971). The evil effect of this belief is that it makes discussion impossible. It diverts attention from the important question of what is the truth, what are the facts, and what can we learn from them, to the comparatively trivial question of motives in asking such questions and interpreting the answers. It leads to a belief that only people who already share a framework of assumptions can hope to reach agreement in a rational discussion. This sounds plausible and reasonable, but has a terrible divisive effect. It breaks mankind into mutually exclusive ideological groups who cannot discuss with one another, only fight each other.

> 'It ignores the likelihood that our western civilization is itself the result of the confrontation between societies who had no common "framework" – the Greeks and their neighbours, then the Greeks and the Romans, Romans and Jews and Germanic peoples, and later still, Christians and Moslems.'

It rests on a false assumption – that truth can be discovered only by eliminating bias and prejudice. Popper shows that this is impossible. Everybody is biased, prejudiced, and interested (in both senses of the word). The fact that, in scientific discussion, for example, and even in courts of law, we can approximate to the truth, is due to the public nature of the discussions, not to lack of bias in the participants. It is on the contrary an advocate's job to be biased. We all know how, though knowing ourselves wrong, we can stick to our position in a private argument and just say 'well, I don't agree'. But in the presence of several onlookers, even if they play no part in the discussion, it is far more difficult to hold on to a logically losing position. We know that somebody is going to say 'It's no good. Admit you are wrong'. Freedom and publicity of discussion, not lack of bias, are the pathways to the truth.

Following on from this and fundamental to Popper's philosophy is the importance of criticism. Some of Popper's ideas have filtered, often in a somewhat garbled form, into popular thought and have had some influence; but some of the most important remain known only to the few people who have studied his works in detail. The idea of criticism as the source of the growth of knowledge is one of these.

Criticism is one of the functions of language and, in evolutionary terms, probably the most recent. The first two functions – expression of feeling, alerting calls and signals – are possessed by many animals. For these, even in man, words are not necessary. The chewing of gum or the puffing at a pipe can say: 'I am not worried' or 'I don't care' and in so saying often tell a lie. A third function, description, is possessed perhaps in rudimentary fashion by some animals. Bees seem to be able to tell each other where nectar is to be found. This descriptive function introduces the standard: true or false. Criticism is the fourth function and is peculiar to man. It arises from the third. The way to the nectar is disputed or there is more of it over there. This critical function introduces the idea of validity in argument and it does require words (see O.K. 235).

Knowledge grows by criticism, by the weeding out of

wrong ideas, just as the species of animals and plants develop by the elimination of maladjusted ones, and skills by the elimination of useless movements and habits. It is a case of the survival of the fittest – in ideas, organisms, and techniques – as a result of the getting rid of the unfit.

The problem of induction

I must substantiate this view and emphasise its far-reaching consequences for human thought by going back to David Hume and the problem of induction. Until Hume demolished the idea in his *Treatise on Human Nature*, published in instalments from 1737 to 1740, it was generally agreed that the rationality of science depended on the process of induction, that is of making generalisations from a limited number of facts. We observe that the sun rises every morning and we conclude from this that it will rise again tomorrow and every other morning – the more frequent the observation, the more secure the generalisation. Hume showed that the logical process was not valid, that there is no *reason* for generalising in this way; and so scientific laws derived in this way could not be said to be founded on reason and experience.

Having established that because A follows B a hundred times there is no *reason* to suppose that on the 101st occasion A will again follow B, Hume fell back on a weaker, psychological, theory. It was that, although there is no reason to suppose this, it is in fact what we all do. We observe repetitions and then act on the assumption that they will go on happening. In spite of its logical invalidity, induction is indispensible in practical life. We live by relying on the continuation of repetition. Association strengthened by repetition is the main mechanism of our intellect, by which we live and act.

So we are left with a paradox – even our intellect (not just our emotions or intuition) does not work rationally. The pre-dawn human sacrifices of the Aztecs provide a chilling example of the consequences of an unquestioning belief in association. The sun invariably rose after the sacrifice; the practice therefore had to go on to ensure that it would continue to rise every morning.

I am not going to give Hume's arguments for rejecting induction because they are intertwined, as was the Aztec reasoning, with ideas about causation; and this complicates the matter. But one can easily imagine how he came to be led towards his conclusion; for, in practice, repetitions do not always occur. Rain may follow the dawn on six days of the week, but this makes it less rather than more likely that there will be rain on the seventh day. Bertrand Russell (1946) said of Hume that he developed to its logical conclusion the empirical philosophy of Locke and Berkeley and, by making it 'self-consistent, made it incredible'. British empiricist philosophers from then on, according to Russell, preferred to reject Hume's scepticism without ever refuting it, while German philosophers simply ignored it. Hume himself said that his treatise 'fell dead-born from the press'. Hume's rational scepticism was ignored and smothered by Rousseau's romantic irrationalism. 'Rousseau was mad but influential', was Russell's comment, 'Hume was sane but had no followers.'

Nevertheless Hume's success in apparently proving that experience and reason have no necessary connection with one another, that there is no such thing as rational belief, was 'an intellectual time-bomb which after sizzling away for two hundred years has only just gone off', according to Lord (Kenneth) Clark. If not even science was rational the way was clear for mysticism. To quote Russell again:

The growth of unreason throughout the nineteenth century and what has passed of the twentieth is a natural sequel to Hume's destruction of empiricism. It is, therefore, important to discover whether there is an answer to Hume within the framework of a philosophy that is wholly or mainly empirical . . . If not, there is no intellectual difference between sanity and insanity, the lunatic who believes he is a poached egg is to be condemned solely on the grounds that he is in a minority. This is a desperate point of view and it must be *hoped* [my italics] that there is some way of escaping from it.

I shall take up in Chapter 6 Hume's psychological theory and give Popper's answer to it. The mistaken quest for certainty was the factor that misled those rationalist philosophers who genuinely sought a solution. Russell (1948) recognised the fact of uncertainty. With a characteristically homely comparison, he put it like this: 'All knowledge is in some degree doubtful, and we cannot say what degree of doubtfulness makes it cease to be knowledge, any more that we can say how much loss of hair makes a man bald.' Possibly he was diverted by the vividness of his own imagery into asking, by implication, the wrong question. For it is not a matter of defining the word knowledge but, as we shall see, of ranking approximations to the truth. The search for a solution within an empirical philosophy was also misleading. The answer is rational but not empirical.

It was when Popper considered the impact made by Einstein on Newton's theory of gravitation that he realised that the solution lay in this very uncertainty about our knowledge of the external world. Newton's theory had been – still is – so astonishingly successful that the problem always seemed to be how to explain man's ability to know about the universe so exactly. The fact that Einstein's totally different theory explained some observations better than did Newton's made Popper realise that both are theories – hypotheses, not facts. This thought then led to Popper's solution of the problem of induction. This was not the disproving of induction. That had already been done by Hume two centuries before, to his and Russell's and many others' satisfaction. It was to explain how rational action is nevertheless possible, how we can be reasonably sure that the man who believes he is a poached egg is wrong.

Popper's solution to this important problem is easily explained. He simply denied that we do act inductively on the assumption that repetitions will go on recurring. We do not act upon the assumption that the future will be the same as the past (when we are behaving rationally) but upon the best-tested theory – the theory for which we have the best *reasons* for believing that it is the nearest to the truth (O.K.95). It is true that we act upon the assumption that the sun will rise tomorrow; but this is not only because it rose today and yesterday, but because it is the best theory. If we were to believe that another celestial body was going to pass near the earth in such a way as to stop its rotation, then we should act on the assumption that the sun would not rise or not set, whichever the best theory might predict. In fact the sixteenth century mariner exploring uncharted seas did not assume that because he saw no land for twenty days on end that he would never see land again. On the contrary. Bertrand Russell (1946), using one of his favourite food examples, said: 'I see an apple, past experience makes me expect that it will taste like an apple, and not like roast beef; but there is no rational justification for this expectation.' Popper's answer to this would be that we expect the apple to taste of apple not only because of past experience but because it is the best theory. Changing to a less fantastic example: if we are told that what looks like a ripe apple is in fact unripe or over-ripe or riddled with maggots we should expect it not to taste like a good ripe apple. Our expectations are certainly not based only on past experience.

This is all there is to it. Popper is saying that we do not act inductively – at any rate when we are using our reason – but on the best available theory whether it involves repetitions or not.

To sum up: the process that *looks* like induction is really one of choosing the theory that is best supported by reason. It is one of a number of similar conceptual illusions. I have already mentioned tunnel-vision or muddle looking like conspiracy. Another is natural selection, which looks like instruction. It looks as though the giraffe acquired its long neck because its ancestors wanted to nibble higher branches and taught their young to stretch their necks and *they* taught their young likewise. What actually happened, we now believe, was that those pre-giraffes with longer than average necks survived better because they could nibble higher; and, where the longer neck was an hereditary variant, *their* progeny again survived better and so on. I mention two more of these conceptual illusions in Chapter 6.

The demarcation of science

One of Popper's earliest philosophical innovations was to suggest a line of demarcation between science and non-science or metaphysics. It was that a scientific theory is, in principle, capable of being shown to be false. The impetus that led him to reverse what had hitherto been the generally accepted view that scientific theories could be confirmed by observations was provided by a number of friends of his youth who were admirers of either Marx, Freud, or Adler.

> These theories appeared to be able to explain practically everything that happened within the fields to which they referred. The study of them seemed to have the effect of an intellectual conversion or revelation, opening your eyes to a new truth hidden from those not yet initiated. Once your eyes were opened you saw confirming instances everywhere: the world was full of *verifications* of the theory. Whatever happened always confirmed it. Thus the truth appeared manifest; and unbelievers were clearly people who did not want to see the manifest truth, either because it was against their class interest, or because of their repressions which were still 'unanalysed' and crying loud for treatment. (C.R.34)

Popper was impressed by his observation that 'a Marxist could not open a newspaper without finding on every page confirming evidence for his interpretation of history' and that Freudian analysts found that their theories were 'constantly verified by their "clinical observations"'. He realised that the great appeal of these theories was that they enabled one 'to know in advance', as Bryan Magee (1973) puts it, 'that whatever happens one will be able to understand it'. At about the same time, in 1919, he heard that Einstein had said that observation failed to show the shift to the red of the lines of the spectrum as he had predicted, 'then the general theory of relativity will be untenable'. Einstein would regard his own theory as untenable if it should fail in certain tests. This, Popper realised, was the true attitude of science. (U.Q.38)

In Popper's view all organisms are endowed with propensities, expectations, one could call them rudimentary theories. The newborn child expects to be fed and cared for. But the expectations are not necessarily fulfilled and this leads to problems, a gap between theory and practice. We survive by learning to solve problems, and we do this by modifying our conjectures. 'The new solution, new behaviour, new theory, may work; or it may fail. Thus we learn by trial and error, or, more precisely, by tentative solutions and their elimination if they prove erroneous.' This method is used by even the most primitive of animals; but *its* theories *are* its behaviour, and if they are wrong it succumbs. But there is a most important difference between what an amoeba does and what a scientist does. In a radio conversation with Bryan Magee, Popper explained it like this:

> On the pre-scientific level we hate the very idea that we may be mistaken. So we cling dogmatically to our conjectures as long as possible. On the scientific level, we systematically search for our mistakes. This is the great thing; we are consciously critical in order to detect our errors. Thus on the pre-scientific level we are often ourselves destroyed, eliminated with our false theories. On the scientific level, we systematically try to eliminate our false theories, we try to let our false theories die in our stead. This is the critical method of error elimination. It is the method of science. It presupposes that we can look at our theories critically, as something outside ourselves. They are not any longer our subjective beliefs [World 2, see page 25]. They are our objective conjectures [World 3].
>
> (*Modern British Philosophy*)

Popper sums up the general picture of science as follows:

We choose some interesting problem. We propose a bold theory as a tentative solution. We try our best to criticise the theory; and this means that we try to refute it. If we succeed in our refutation, then we try to produce a new theory, which we shall again criticise, and so on . . . The whole procedure can be summed up by the words: bold conjectures, controlled by severe criticism which includes severe tests. And criticism, and tests, are attempted refutations (Magee, 1971).

Thus a theory cannot be proved, it can only be disproved. But the more it stands up to attempts to refute it, the more secure it becomes, although it can never be regarded as certain. Popper encourages the formulation of theories in such a form as to say: 'If such and such experiment were performed with such and such a result then the theory would fail.' Scientific theories, as it were, forbid certain eventualities; and 'the more a theory forbids the more it tells us'. While 'a theory which cannot clash with any possible or conceivable event is . . . outside science'. (U.Q.41)

To see straight away what is implied by this criterion of demarcation for science, one can look at the continuing controversy on intelligence (measured by I.Q.) and race. Professor Hans Eysenck, prominent among the protagonists, has recently stated, in an article in *New Scientist* (1979) that the basis of the psychologists' case is 'the theory that all cognitive performances are to a variable degree a function of a single underlying ability (intelligence or g) . . . ' Now this theory is so imprecise that one cannot conceive of any observation or experiment that could refute it. Yet endless discussion proceeds, looking like scientific argument and involving abstruse mathematics, of what is, by Popper's criterion, metaphysics.

Popper cannot identify the process whereby we get the hunches, or whatever, that form the theories that have to be tested – 'New ideas have a striking similarity to genetic mutations' (S.B.54) – but he does suggest that they are not arrived at by induction. This is because the observation of repetitions is the result not the cause of the theory. We make a guess that A may be followed by B and then we watch out and see if it is so. We do not go and observe with a blank mind. We have expectations and then we observe to see whether they are confirmed.

A good example of the contrast between the inductive approach and the Popperian view of science is provided by the attitudes of Francis Bacon and Galileo in the seventeenth century. Bacon taught that men must rid their minds of prejudices (theories) and just go and observe and, as it were, 'read the open book of Nature'. Galileo realised that all is interpretation, that we have to arrive at the correct interpretation of what we appear to see. He was full of admiration for the astronomers Copernicus and Kepler because they refused to believe what they saw. Their eyes told them that the sun goes round the earth. Anybody can see it. You just go and look. Copernicus preferred to believe his reason which told him that this was an illusion.

The distinguished neuro-physiologist, Sir John Eccles (co-author with Popper of *The Self and Its Brain*), has recorded his personal experience of conversion to the Popperian view of science. At the time when he first met Popper, he was in a state of depression, desperately clinging to a theory he had proposed about the mechanism of nervous transmission which, in his heart of hearts, he had begun to suspect was wrong. Popper persuaded him that it was no disgrace to have one's hypotheses refuted. Indeed this was the means by which science advances. Encouraged by this view, he proceeded to join the 'killing' of his own 'brain-child' and to assist in the advancement of the theory of his rivals. 'It was in this most personal manner', Eccles wrote, 'that I experienced the great liberating power of Popper's teachings on scientific method.' (*The Philosophy of Karl Popper*)

This story contrasts strongly with what happens in politics where the behaviour of politicians, civil servants, and political parties resembles much more the amoeba than the Popperian scientist. They can seldom admit themselves to have been wrong and they tend to bind themselves to particular solutions rather than to solving problems.

Richard Crossman relates in his diaries how he asked Mr Callaghan, then Home Secretary, why it was that he was now in April (1969) proposing an obviously sensible reform in respect of immigration which he had himself opposed in the previous October. What had made the difference? The answer was that the chief immigration officer had been shifted. Similarly, in his analysis of the way in which three municipal authorities dealt with their transport problems, John Grant showed how only by getting rid of the leading participants – in one case by defeat at the polls, in another by the death of the City Engineer – could the policy be changed. In the third case, where both party and leading actors survived, the road-building ambitions of the 1960s were only chipped away bit by bit.

Popper's great innovation, then, is that human knowledge, especially scientific knowledge, depends upon criticism for its advances. This idea is linked with another, which is also contrary to a popular saw – that you can never prove a negative. On the contrary, if you are talking about general propositions and theories, negatives are the only things you *can* prove. (The confusion arises from the fact that the opposite is true of singular events.) As Popper puts it: 'No number of sightings of white swans can establish the theory that all swans are white; but the first observation of a black swan can refute it' – assuming of course that the total number of swans in the world is not known.

I think it is fair to say that Popper's formulation of the process of growth of scientific knowledge is now generally accepted by natural scientists themselves. It is interesting to compare it with what had immediately preceded it, the theory held by the logical positivists that any theory that could not in principle be confirmed, was not just non-science but nonsense. In Popper's view what is non-science, as defined by his subtly different criterion, is not necessarily nonsense. Metaphysical ideas can, with the growth of knowledge, become scientific theories. To take a fantastic example, a century ago the theory that the moon was made of green cheese was metaphysical. There was no possible way of proving it false. Now it could be considered a scientific theory that has been conclusively disproved. Or, as a realistic example, take the recently publicised theory that anorexia nervosa (complete loss of appetite and consequent severe loss of weight, usually in adolescent girls or young women) is caused by a fear of reaching maturity. Now this may or may not be true; but it would be difficult to put this hypothesis into a form such that it, or its logical consequences, could be refuted. I do not deny that it may be a helpful idea to have in one's mind when dealing with a particular case. But there is a great danger in *believing* it to be a fact. For such a belief will tend to make one disregard other evidence, especially any statements by the patient herself, which appear to contradict it.

Science is not necessarily connected with microscopes and electronic machinery. It is a method of acquiring knowledge. What is called scientific knowledge has been laboriously built up over the years and thoroughly tested but is *not* certain. It includes social as well as physical science. Theories which are not testable and, therefore, do not belong to science on Popper's criterion, may be interesting and fruitful – as for example Marxism and psychoanalysis – but cannot command a degree of reliance in any way approaching that commanded by scientific theories that have stood up to tests.

In concluding this chapter I must emphasise the fact that the growth of scientific knowledge depends on the publication of theories and on freedom of speech in criticising them. Technology may thrive in secrecy and under tyranny but science cannot. Two groups of people are required for the growth of knowledge: those putting forward the theories and the critics, who may or may not be experts of some sort themselves, trying to find fault with the theories.

2

Three worlds

This chapter is devoted to another Popper innovation – a more recent one – which has far-reaching implications for psychology and all aspects of human behaviour. Hitherto controversy has ranged around the mind–body problems with such questions as: Is mind something separate from body? Does mind control body or vice versa? Or is mind an illusion, an epiphenomenon, something like the locomotive's whistle that has no effect on the working of the body-machine? (The analogy is T. H. Huxley's and represents what he believed to be the case.)

In tackling this question, Popper distinguishes between two problems which have tended to be telescoped into one. The first he called Descartes's problem, and he stated it like this:

> How can it be that such things as states of mind – volitions, feelings, expectations – influence or control the physical movements of our limbs? (O.K. 231)

The second he called Compton's problem because it had first caught his attention in a published lecture by the American physicist-philosopher, Arthur Holly Compton. Unlike Descartes's problem, it had not been appreciated by philosophers of the past, Popper says. If they saw it at all, they saw it only dimly. He stated this general problem in terms of the specific problem Compton himself had posed, namely how to explain the faith of his Yale audience that he would return from Italy to lecture to them at the time and date advertised, bearing in mind that, viewed as a physical event, it was a fantastically improbable one. So the problem, as Popper puts it, is this:

There are such things as letters accepting a proposal to lecture, and public announcements of intentions; publicly declared aims and purposes; general moral rules. Each of these . . . has a certain content or meaning, which remains invariant if we translate it or reformulate it. Thus *this content or meaning is quite abstract*. Yet it can control – perhaps by way of a short cryptic entry in a diary – the physical movements of a man in such a way as to steer him back from Italy to Connecticut. How can this be? (O.K. 230)

Popper not only affirms the separate existence (and power) of mind, but points out the existence of a third reality, the world of the *products* of the human mind. He is thus not merely a dualist but a pluralist. World I, in his scheme of things, is the material world which includes brains and also physical forces such as magnetism and gravitation. World 2 is the world of consciousness, or mental events. Descartes's problem is the problem of how World 2 acts on World 1. In addition there is World 3, consisting of art, music, moral obligations, ideas, problems, theories (true and false), which have been published or spoken or written down – objective as opposed to subjective knowledge. Compton's problem is thus the question of how World 3 acts upon World 1. Although produced by human·minds, World 3 is no longer 'within' minds. Popper is making the distinction between thoughts (World 2) and the externalised results of thoughts (World 3). (O.K. 153 and S.B. 38)

His tentative solution to both the problems he defines is given in a paper called 'Of Clouds and Clocks' (O.K. 206). I cannot even sketch it here. I raise the matter only to emphasise the reality and the power in all our lives of World 3. In the form of theories, proposals, and plans, World 3 items will loom large in the rest of this book.

It is Popper's conjecture that World 3 developed hand in hand with World 2, and it was language that made both possible. There is no mind, no consciousness, he conjectures, or at any rate no self-consciousness, without the products of mind.

The above paragraph may be dismissed as metaphysics.

There is no conceivable way of proving these conjectures false. But it is not hard to show that World 3 objects exist. They are abstract but real. That they are abstract is shown by the fact that they have no location in space. 'Where is the English language?' is a meaningless question. Their reality is demonstrated by their power, by way of World 2, to influence World I. Popper exemplifies this by postulating two variants of a hypothetical disaster, for example nuclear holocaust. In both all adult humans die and just a few children survive. The difference is that in one case the libraries survive and in the other all human artefacts are destroyed. In the first case, one can imagine that in a few generations civilisation might be rebuilt; in the second the human race must be set back 30,000 years. It makes no difference what material form the recorded knowledge takes. Instead of libraries it could be magnetic tapes with the appropriate means of reproducing them. All that matters is that they should be intelligible to the survivors.

Or take a less hypothetical example of the power of a message, the public notice of a theatrical performance, pop concert, or football match. Those printed words in newspaper or poster will in a real sense cause the movement of hundreds or thousands of people from their homes to the place named. The effect is independent of the physical ink and paper, being the same whether printed in capitals or lower case, English or French, broadcast by radio or public address, provided only that the minds (World 2) can grasp it.

Two points must be emphasised. (1) Abstract ideas have this power to change the material world only when they become objective, World 3, public knowledge as opposed to private thoughts; and (2) their power to affect World I is exerted only via World 2. World 3 objects, the products of human minds, have to be grasped again by human minds before they can produce results in World 1. A book is of itself a powerless World I object. But if its *message* (World 3) is grasped in the mind (World 2) of a reader (World I) that reader may in consequence take action which he would not otherwise have taken. That action is therefore caused or partly caused by a World 3 object.

It is worth pointing out the reality of World 3 objects as compared to something like a corporate spirit. A group of people, it can be a committee or a team, may be said to have a life over and above the lives of its members. But that life or spirit depends on its members being alive. Shoot them all and there is nothing left of the spirit. But, though Shakespeare is very long dead, his plays live on and influence us to this day.

Philosophers are well known to be obsessed with Plato and at the drop of a hat will quote Whitehead's defeatest view that the most anybody can hope to do is to write 'footnotes to Plato'. Inevitably therefore Popper's World 3 has been written off in some academic circles as a re-hash of Plato's forms, which were conceived as a kind of pure essence or distillation of crude impure realities. They were of divine origin and changeless. Popper's World 3 objects are man-made and constantly being modified, corrected, added to. Furthermore Plato's forms were powerless in the physical world; Popper's World 3 has changed the face of the earth. (I am referring to the fact that the immense physical changes brought about by man have been the consequence of theorising and grasping of theories and of the growth of human knowledge.) Finally Popper, points out, World 3 is to some extent autonomous. Man invented the natural numbers 1, 2, 3 etc., but he did not decide that the sequence of numbers should contain an irregular number of prime numbers nor that every even number should be the sum of two primes. Similarly a theory often contains within itself implications that were unintended by its author. A theory, as it were, generates its own sub-theories.

Nevertheless, Popper has to justify his pluralism against conventional monist theories such as the one that mental events are brain processes which would take place anyway whether conscious or not. This implies that the fact of their being conscious has no material effect. Popper's argument is in essence an evolutionary one and this is what makes the footnotes-to-Plato school look a bit silly. For centuries philosophers laboured under what H. G. Wells called 'that fantastically precise misconception' that the world had been created quite suddenly in the year 4004 B.C. (although it was uncertain whether in the spring or the autumn of that year). Plato's misconception would have been less precise; but he would not have taken into account a world without life. We with our vastly wider horizon have to consider the advantages of each change, in particular the change from unconscious life to consciousness.

The biological function of World 2, in Popper's view, lies in its ability to 'produce theories and conscious anticipations of impending events' and to grasp World 3. That is, the biological function of conscious minds (as opposed to unconscious brain processes) is to seek, select, interpret, and understand the ideas first formed in other people's minds and then by some means made publicly available, and to add to them. It is the main biological function of World 3 to make it possible for these ideas to be rejected – 'to let our theories die in our stead' (S. B. 138). Language made it possible for World 2 ideas to be externalised, made objective, and thus shared, built on, and criticised. We have already seen how knowledge grows by criticism. You cannot criticise an idea in somebody else's mind until it has been transformed from a mental event (World 2) into a public World 3 object, by being spoken or written down. It is not even very easy to criticise an idea in one's own mind, as most of us discover when we come to explain to somebody else or to defend what, up to that moment, had seemed to be a good idea. As Popper says: 'the very small difference between *thinking* (in the sense of acting on the assumption) "today is Saturday" and *saying* "today is Saturday" makes a tremendous difference from the point of view of the possibility of criticism' (S.B. 451). In the long run, therefore, the biological advantage of consciousness is that it makes possible the cumulative growth of knowledge.

The two groups of psychological theory which have had the greatest impact on human thought in this century (and form the subjects of Chapters 5 and 6) tend to discount the importance of consciousness, assuming almost that 'the true mind of man is in the unconscious, as if man were most absent-minded when he is most attentive', as Arthur Little put it. Because they discount consciousness, they necessarily ignore the question of its function, and of the biological advantage conferred by it. The importance of Popper's World 3 concept is that it draws attention to this major power in our lives that popular psychologies leave totally out of account, the stuff that consciousness works on.

A few bacteria inoculated into a suitable culture medium may increase in numbers to 3 or 400 million organisms per millilitre of medium in some twelve hours. After a further forty-eight hours they may all be dead, having used up all the nourishment and poisoned their own environment. In the absence of periodic wars and pestilences the same sort of fate may threaten the human race. Bacteria can respond only to 'routine' stimuli; but our consciousness and ability to theorize offer at least a hope that we may escape the otherwise inevitable. Toynbee stressed that it was our ability to learn from history that might prevent our civilization from going the way of its predecessors; but in more precise, Popperian terms, this ability to learn from history is an aspect of our ability to 'grasp World 3'. It depends on the reality of Worlds 2 and 3.

In *The Self and Its Brain* (p. 549) Popper gives what amounts to a proof that World 1, the material world, cannot be all that there is, that no material object could achieve what the mind does achieve. He uses Euclid's proof that the series of prime numbers is infinite and shows how such a proof must belong solely to Worlds 2 and 3, essentially because you cannot make a material model of infinity.

I end this chapter, in a parallel vein, with a kind of mathematical demonstration both of the superiority of conscious reasoning over unconscious, genetic, programming, and of the importance of institutions. It amounts also to a refutation of what some ethologists are always telling us, if not in so many words, that we should do what chimpanzees do. It comes from Richard Dawkins's most important book *The Selfish Gene*. His dominating theme is that natural selection operates at the level of the gene (or at any rate a short section of DNA) rather than on the individual, group, or species, because the gene is the thing that is replicated. 'This is not a theory; it is not even an observed fact; it is a tautology', he says. It amounts to saying that what survives best survives best.

Dawkins combines this idea with the concept, invented

by Professor John Maynard Smith, of *evolutionary stable strategy* (ESS), which is best explained by the simplest example Dawkins quotes. He supposes an animal which inherits a tendency to behave either as a 'hawk' or a 'dove'. When an asset such as a piece of territory or a female is in dispute, a 'hawk' will attack, retreating only if seriously hurt, while a 'dove' will stand and stare, never hurting his opponent and, if attacked, he will retreat before he himself is hurt. Maynard Smith allots scores, pay–offs, for each kind of confrontation, based on an assessment of the numbers of the animals' genes that are likely to survive (in itself and its relatives). Winning a fight scores +50 and serious injury costs − 100. There is also a cost, − 10, for wasting time, trying to stare out the opponent (which, for example for a small bird in a cold climate, might be lethal to itself or its offspring waiting to be fed). A dove that wins therefore scores 40 (+50 −10). Now if all are doves there is an unstable situation, because one mutant or invading hawk has a huge initial advantage. Hawk genes then spread rapidly at first until there is a good chance of any one hawk having to fight another. Similar considerations apply to all-hawk populations, because a lone dove, although he scores zero in any encounter, does much better than the average hawk who loses one to every one that he wins (his average score is a half of +50 −100 = −25). Maynard Smith's idea is that a stable population in respect of this one characteristic will ultimately evolve. Simple arithmetic shows that it will have 7 hawks to every 5 doves (on these scores). In such an ESS the average pay–off per confrontation is $6\frac{1}{4}$.

The important thing is that this pay–off is less than the average score (15) which would be obtained by an, albeit unstable, all–dove population. Thus the blind, unconscious forces achieve a stability which is by no means the best of all possible worlds. Conscious calculation can arrive at a better solution and all that is needed is an institution to enforce it, namely the outlawing of hawkishness. Interestingly enough, it can even tolerate a little law-breaking. For an occasional outburst of hawkishness results in an even better average score, $16\frac{2}{3}$ for one hawk to every 5 doves!

3

Forms of unreason

'Socrates's great equalitarian and liberating idea that it is possible to reason with a slave, and that there is an intellectual link between man and man, a medium of universal understanding, namely, "reason".' O.S., i, 132

My favourite chapter in the whole of Popper's writing is the last but one in *The Open Society* where he explores the kind of borderland between reason and faith in reason, in a way which I have found of lasting value and comfort. The chapter begins with the observation that Marx was a rationalist, but that the consequence of his work and influence has been an undermining of belief in reason. Rationalism has been assaulted both from the Left – by the Marxist doctrine that opinions are determined by class interest – and also from the Right by Hegel's doctrine that ideas are determined by national interest. 'This is why', says Popper, 'the conflict between rationalism and irrationalism has become the most important intellectual, and perhaps even moral, issue of our time' (O.S., ii, 224).

Rationalism in Popper's sense implies an attitude of reasonableness, of 'I may be wrong and you may be right, and by an effort we may get nearer the truth'. He is at pains to emphasise that this attitude cannot itself be justified by reason, it cannot be proved. It is more akin to a moral attitude. 'For the question whether to adopt rationalism or irrationalism will deeply affect our whole attitude to other men, and towards the problems of social life.' (O.S.,ii, 232). He proceeds to justify his choice of rationalism mainly by looking at its opposite. What he calls 'irrationalism' is the attitude of those who insist that 'human nature' is not rational. They may recognise reason and scientific method as useful tools to serve certain ends; but these very ends will be irrational because the 'deep motives' of human action are emotional and not amenable to reason. Further, because of this and because so few people are capable of serious argument, the majority, they say, can only be tackled by an appeal to their emotions and passions rather than to their reason.

Irrationalism, since it is not bound by any rules or consistency, may be combined with any kind of belief including a belief in the brotherhood of man; but the irrationalist's belief that emotions and passions rather than reason are the mainspring of human action tend to lead to an appeal to violence and brute force as the ultimate arbiter in any dispute. Bertrand Russell had written: 'Rationality . . . is of supreme importance . . . not only in ages in which it easily prevails, but even more, in those less fortunate times in which it is despised and rejected as the vain dream of men who lack the virility to kill where they cannot agree.' With what he calls a harmless test case Popper shows that even the most constructive emotion, love, is usually unable to decide a conflict. Tom likes the theatre and Dick likes dancing. Tom lovingly insists on going to a dance while Dick wants, for Tom's sake, to go to the theatre (O.S., ii, 236).

'Starvation lunches' organised to help the underfed millions in the poorest countries of the world are probably a case in point. The idea that we should fast for this purpose is founded on generous emotions but bad reason. If the amount we eat has anything to do with providing more for Bangladesh, we would be more likely to help by eating more. For it is increased demand for their exports, rather than reduced demand, that is most likely to help them.

The adoption of rationalism implies, Popper says, a commitment to a common language of reason, and establishes a kind of moral obligation to use it with clarity and in such a way that it retain its function as a vehicle of argument. He inveighs against the tendency to regard language as a means of self-expression rather than a means of communication, and sees this misuse as part of the revolt against reason.

As a short digression to emphasise the point of clarity of language, here is Richard Asher, a medical lecturer of genius, talking to a meeting of psychiatrists (a profession not renowned for clarity):

> If for a moment we consider the dynamic formulation of both objective and subjective thought–fantasy, the cognitive functions can easily become projected into an integrated but psychically barren wish–fulfilment.

The reader will be relieved to know that he went on:

> That last high–sounding sentence, as I hope you noticed, has no meaning whatsoever and is pure nonsense; but I wrote it to demonstrate that, with the aid of abstract terms, it is easy to parade such a brave show of words in front of one's thoughts that it is extremely difficult to see if there *is* any idea behind them; and it is equally easy to take a small idea and wrap around it such a mantle of language that it can dazzle the unwary into applause.

That was a spoof; but here is a definition, quoted by June Lait and given, apparently in all seriousness, by the British Association of Social Workers:

> Social work is the purposeful and ethical application of personal skills in interpersonal relationships directed towards enhancing the personal and social functioning of an individual, family, group, or neighbourhood, which necessarily involves using evidence obtained from practice to help create a social environment conducive to the well being of all.

Because the roots of reason lie in discussion and dialogue, there is implicit in rationalism a recognition of a common humanity. A cat can look at a king. An ignorant non–intellectual may put his finger on a professor's mistake. Criticism is the source of the advance of knowledge, and it can come from anybody. In his fascinating book on why things don't fall down, Professor J. E. Gordon tells how he 'spent a whole evening in Cambridge trying to explain to two scientists of really shattering eminence and world-wide fame the basic difference between stress and strain and strength and stiffness' (A–level physics) in connection with a project about which they were advising the government. And he was not certain how far he was successful. I mention this not to jeer at the ignorance of our betters, but to emphasise that nobody knows everything, even about the subject he is supposed to be expert in, and so everybody needs to be subject to criticism.

The tendency of rationalism is thus anti-authoritarian, anti-élitist (to use the modern expression, though there is a regrettable tendency for this to mean anti-anybody with any kind of skill), and non-divisive. It is also equalitarian in the sense in which we talk of equality before the law. As Popper says: 'It cannot be denied that human individuals are . . . in very many respects unequal, nor . . . that this inequality is in many respects highly desirable.' But this has nothing to do with political rights, with how you decide to treat people. 'Equality before the law is not a fact but a political demand based upon a moral decision; and it is quite independent of the theory – which is probably false – that "all men are born equal"' (O.S., ii, 234). Individual irrationalists may adopt these attitudes which are consequences of rationalist faith; but rationalists, if they are consistent, *must* adopt them.

Rationalism in Popper's sense combines reason in the sense of argument and discussion – what is sometimes called 'intellectualism' – with observation of the real world, learning by experience – empiricism. (But he is a follower of Immanuel Kant to the extent that he rejects 'naive empiricism', what he calls the bucket theory of mind, which sees the mind as a passive collector of perceptions.) Rationalism has to be distinguished, he says, from 'pseudo-rationalism' as typified by Plato's remark in the *Timaeus* that 'reason is shared only by the gods and by very few men'. Popper denounces this attitude as: 'This authoritarian intellectualism, this belief in the possession of an infallible instrument of discovery . . . this failure to distinguish between a man's intellectual powers and his indebtedness to others for all he can possibly know or understand' (O.S., ii, 227). His view is that 'We not only owe our reason to others, but we can never excel others in our reasonableness in a way that would establish a claim to authority' (ibid., 226)

The rest of this chapter is devoted to three particular departures from reason which have a powerful influence on modern thought.

Holism

What Popper calls *holism* is the theory that the proper way of carrying out reforms is to treat the thing reformed – whether nation, segment of society, large area of city, or even (I would add) human patient – as a whole and change it as a whole. One alternative, if not the only one, is the theory he made explicit more than thirty years ago and called (perhaps rather unhappily) 'piecemeal social engineering'. Here the method is: first to identify the problem, to state preferably in writing (so that it can be objectively criticised) what is the abuse or unfairness or inefficiency to be corrected and what is the object to be achieved; then to suggest a tentative solution – a 'theory' – followed by attempts to guess in advance what will be the undesirable consequences of putting the solution into practice and the finding of ways of preventing or minimising them. The piecemeal planner is modest in his approach. 'Like Socrates, he knows how little he knows.' He knows that we can learn only from our mistakes. He lays down criteria in advance for the judging of success or failure and takes steps to look out for unanticipated, but inevitable, snags or 'side effects'. He will be careful not to make simultaneously more changes than he can hope to keep track of, in order to be sure that when things go wrong (as he must expect they will) he can know what is causing what.

A nice example of the best laid plans of men going wrong in the most unexpected way is provided by a case quoted by Professor Geoffrey Broadbent of some efficient planning of a new law court building. There was a gross reduction in space 'wasted' on corridors and stairways and thus in the distances which people had to walk. But the consequence of 'the lack of dim corners where informal conferences and settlements can take place meant that many more cases came to trial . . . and the court calendars became overloaded'.

The holist disparages the piecemeal method as lacking

boldness. In his view society is usually at fault 'from its roots'. A radical solution is needed and this must involve changing things as a whole. The first difficulty arises here. For while it is easy for people to agree on what the problems are – what the wrongs are that need righting – it is virtually impossible for people to agree on the ideal of how things should be. Each has his own idea of Utopia and one man's meat is truly another's poison.

It may sometimes seem that there is only a theoretical difference between the two methods. For the scope of a piecemeal reform may be very great and that of the holist-in-spirit will usually be less than total. The holist can hardly change the language of a society, nor can he immediately change the make-up of its built environment, or the knowledge and skills of its members, three of the most important things in determining how a society functions. Nevertheless the difference in attitude of the two types of reformers makes a profound difference to the outcome. In the first place the holist is committed in principle to the largest possible scope, while the piecemeal planner limits his scope to the minimum necessary. He expects snags and is poised to adjust to them. The holist is committed to the execution of his plan in total. Snags must be brushed aside, a deaf ear turned to complaints. But the bigger the scheme the bigger the snags, and some will be so big as to make the working of the scheme imposible. So impromptu, *piecemeal*, changes will have to be made – 'the notorious phenomenon of *unplanned planning*', as Popper calls it.

As examples of this one may cite the numerous ad hoc changes that have made nonsense of attempts to plan the national economy as a whole: the planned reduction in staffs to economise on public expenditure and then the job-creation scheme to cope with the unemployment it caused; the orders to local authorities to cut their capital expenditure and then the sudden offers to counties (of £5M in the case of Hampshire in 1976/7) to be spent in a hurry on public works (which had just been cancelled) in order to help the resulting unemployment. The sustained campaign to drive small businesses and the self-employed to the wall and now, like Dr Johnson's patron, the encumbering of the survivors with help.

In fact the holist method turns out to be impossible (P.H., Section 24). The reason is that the whole idea depends on regarding human society as an assemblage of machines whose functions and inter-relationships can be known and planned for. But this is false. As Popper says:

> The holistic planner overlooks the fact that it is easy to centralize power but impossible to centralize all that knowledge which is distributed over many individual minds, and whose centralization would be necessary for the wise wielding of centralized power. (P.H., 90)

The critics (and there are many doctors among them), who think that doctors should treat the whole man and not just his illness, make a similar mistake. What they usually mean is that the doctor should take into consideration other aspects, together with the physical. The ones they tend to think of are the psychological, social, and sexual aspects. But these do not make up the whole man, and for any list that might be produced one could always think of an item omitted. The conventional and rational medical attitude, which is that of the piecemeal planner, is first to see if there is a problem at all (is this abnormal or not?), if so, to make a diagnosis, a theory as to what is wrong, to be ready to correct this diagnosis as the case proceeds, to decide whether any treatment is possible or desirable and in deciding on the kind of treatment to take account of all those aspects that seem to be *relevant*. As Richard Asher put it:

> Any reasonable doctor when managing a patient takes into account what his home is like, what sort of family he has, and whether he is rich or poor. If Mr Jones lives in one room with five children, two cats, and a drunken slatternly wife, any sensibile doctor would not order him to rest at home with two-hourly feeds of steamed custard. Nobody would be the slightest bit impressed if anyone explained the obvious thing in a plain way, but if you follow my instructions and 'consider the patient as a psycho-dynamic whole, viewed as a socio-economic unit

integrated within the cultural framework of his environmental and psychobiological relationships' then everybody will be deeply impressed . . . The use of these key words lends an impressive but nebulous air of humane profundity to your utterances and conveys that ordinary doctors are unsympathetic and remote beings with no interest in their patients' feelings.

In a case of acute appendicitis or strangulated hernia, surgical operation must be carried out at once and all other considerations set aside, except for the fitness of the patient for operation. This is one extreme. At the other are the middle-aged ladies who throng G.P.s' surgeries complaining of dizzy turns. Here the doctor has to cast his net wide and often bring in outside help. The difference is that in the first case the patient is not seeking to have his whole life delved into or changed. He only wants the blockage in his guts put right. In the dizzy turn case it is likely that a lot of factors are involved, many of them non-medical, and it is possible that her way of life may need some substantial change. It is clearly silly to assume from the start that every patient needs a radical change, any more than a car with a flat tyre needs a complete overhaul. It is well known among doctors that enthusiasts for the whole-man approach are the first to demand specialists when they themselves or their children are ill. Whole man-ism is for other people.

Perhaps the first difference between holism and the piecemeal approach – the fact that the piecemeal planner begins by formulating as accurately as possible what the problem is, while the holist begins with a pre-conceived 'blue-print' of how things should be – is in practice the most important. To take a comparatively trivial but typical recent example; the change to reporting rainfall in centimetres. The holist approach clearly was: our aim is a clean-sweep. Away with these archaic measures, let us adopt throughout the whole range the system of measurements in use on the continent of Europe. He might have gone as far as to enquire whether there would be any snags in changing from inches, but would be easily persuaded that there would be negligible difficulty. The conversion from one scale to the other is after all a simple ratio. The piecemeal planner on the other hand would start by asking whether there was any problem in continuing to report rainfall in inches. It is inconceivable that he would have found any demand at all for the change. No problem, he would think, means no solution needed; and he would make no change.

I would emphasize that here, as in the case of so many holist-inspired schemes, it is the general public who are put to inconvenience for the sake of trivial advantage to a few experts or bureaucrats. While the continental meteorologist, mapping rainfalls around the world, would equip himself with a ready means of converting inches or any other local measure to centimetres, the British amateur who is casually interested to see whether this has been a wetter year than 1970 is put to some trouble. The same, of course, applies, only more so, to the many other measurements that have been gratuitously changed. One of the factors which led to the swift and almost debate-less making of these changes was the discounting, which is necessary for holists, of individual private knowledge. It is easy, for example, to remember that the normal body temperature, 98.4° on the Fahrenheit scale, is equivalent to 36.6° on the Centigrade (now re-named Celsius) scale. But the individual doctor will have mental pictures of variations from the normal. He will know that in acute appendicitis the temperature is usually a little over 99° F and that if it is as high as 101° F another diagnosis should be suspected. It is not so easy without pencil and paper to translate this kind of knowledge. Similarly with such rules of thumb as 1° F rise in temperature is accompanied, other things being equal, by a rise of pulse rate of about 10 per minute.

It is ironical too that while hurrying to rid us of inches and pounds, which everybody understands, our masters still make us buy our gas in therms, a highly parochial British measure which practically nobody understands. Yet there is an international metric measure of energy which even British people do understand – the kilowatt-hour, the unit by which electricity is sold, the heat given out by the standard one-bar electric fire in one hour. (One therm equals about 29.4 kilowatt-hours). Here is a change which would actually help ordinary people. It would make it much easier then to see whether gas or electricity is the best buy in any particular case.

The holist attitude very readily leads to what I have called solutioneering, a kind of problem shift. Because he does not believe in first considering the question; 'what is the problem to be solved?' he quickly substitutes for the real problem the problem of the implementing of *his* solution. Let us say there is a traffic problem, not clearly formulated. The holist traffic engineer (they usually are holists – their training has taught them that the solution to all traffic problems is to build a new road) plans to build a new road, and the problem becomes how to get it built against the opposition to it, or which is the best route for it. The original problem of what is the best way to deal with the traffic never gets discussed at all.

As I write this (1979) my fellow city councillors and I are being invited by Hampshire County Council to choose between five alternative road schemes ranging in price from £4½ million to £8 million. The problem we are trying to solve is nowhere spelt out in the report. It is just implied that now is the time to do something about the roads in a particular area of the city. One might reasonably assume that we are trying to eliminate bottlenecks and prevent some of the traffic delays which at present do occur. But the causes of the delays are not identified and the five alternatives are not presented as alternative solutions to problems. The one recommended to us retains a roundabout, which is in fact the biggest single obstruction to traffic flow, and it adds two new ones. There is thus a real possibility, which is not considered in the report, needless to say, that the result of spending some £6 million will be that traffic flows even more sluggishly.

Holism has inspired the following recent changes in our national life: the reorganisation of the National Health Service with an additional tier of management (see Chapter 10); the reorganisation of local government with *its* additional administrative tier, obliteration of historic names and boundaries, and creation of new non-communities; the reorganisation of the social services (on the recommendations of the Seebohm report), diluting the skills of children's officers and mental welfare officers by making them take on each others' jobs; the reorganisation of the nursing service (Salmon report), surreptitiously substituting administration for nursing advancement as the reward of a nurse's ambitions; decimalisation and metrication of measurements and money; comprehensive reorganisation of secondary education in a blaze of publicity but simultaneously confused with a stealthy introduction of new and largely untested teaching methods and the quiet dropping of such unifying traditions as the learning of poetry and songs and of Euclidean geometry, that unique discipline combining logic with the appreciation of shape and form; the comprehensive redevelopment of cities (of which more anon) and the building of the motorway network. These are not all complete disasters, perhaps, although all have had very damaging consequences. Had it been generally realised that part of the steam behind all of them was holism, a logically impossible ideal, then the schemes might have been quite different or not carried out at all. Leslie Chapman's *Your Disobedient Servant* must make one suspect that at least part of the enthusiasm in the civil service for reorganisations is related to the fact that they make investigation of past mistakes that much more difficult. A department that has ceased to exist can hardly be brought to book.

It is worth pointing out that none of these schemes was introduced as a result of popular demand. Probably only comprehensive schooling figured in any of the political parties' manifestos. In some cases the schemes went directly against what was well known to be the general wish of the people. Comprehensive urban redevelopment has amounted, almost always, to rebuilding with flats, even if not very high ones. It was well known that almost everybody wanted a house with a garden and this was precisely what most of the destroyed areas consisted of. There was an element of ruthlessness in these schemes – the brainchildren of 'experts' – in that they were foisted on an unwilling country, in some instances without the cases for and against ever being squarely argued in Parliament, and in others (e.g. the abandonment of formal teaching, comprehensive urban development, and the motorway network) without any prior authorisation by Parliament at all.

Occupying a sort of half-way house between holism and what I have called white-swanning is centralisation, that great panacea of our time. Its advantages are obvious at the start, but its disadvantages, which become obvious later, are usually ignored until too late. A nice instance was revealed to me when I was a governor of a comprehensive school. A new classroom block had just been completed; but one room which was intended for the showing of films and television was still lacking its blinds. These had had to be ordered through 'central supply' at county headquarters thirty miles away. The clerk there had looked through his list and found that the cheapest blinds were those obtainable from France. He duly ordered them. They arrived a little late and, not very surprisingly, did not fit the windows. They were sent back and the second lot did not fit either. Less than a mile from the school was a factory for blinds which had hitherto supplied the needs of the area and fitted them with, so far as I was aware, complete satisfaction. In a flash I understood the need for all those juggernauts – to deliver from as far away as possible things that don't fit and take them back again!

Historicism

Often closely allied with holism as an irrational influence in public and private decisions is the theory known as *historicism*, roughly what is also known as historical inevitability. This is the idea that there is a 'tide of history', that 'history' moves under laws analogous to those that keep the moon and the planets on their inevitable courses. The theory is the basis of innumerable myths, of the idea of the chosen people, the second coming, the master race, of peoples and classes carrying out their historic missions. We are actors in a play written by God, or swimmers in the great current of history.

In Marx's view the change from one state of social organisation to the other was inevitable, from feudalism to capitalism to socialism. The most that human action could do was to assist it on its inevitable course, give it a push on its way, as it were. The imagery he used was of the midwife. 'When a society has discovered the natural law that determines its own movement, even then it can neither overleap the natural phases of its evolution, nor shuffle them out of the world by a stroke of the pen. But this much it can do: it can shorten and lessen the birth-pangs.' (From preface to *Das Capital*.) Popper comments that this excellently represents the historicist position. 'Although it teaches neither inactivity nor real fatalism, historicism teaches the futility of any attempt to alter impending changes; a peculiar variety of fatalism, a fatalism in regard to the trends of history, as it were.'

Popper draws attention to a broad distinction between two kinds of prediction in the natural sciences, made from, on the one hand, astronomy and meteorology and, on the other, physics. The first two sciences on the whole enable one to make predictions which, although they may have practical use, do not suggest any action other than evasion. They predict the motions of the heavenly bodies or the weather but there is nothing we can do to change them. The typical prediction from physics, on the other hand, is of the form 'if you *do* so and so then the result will be of such a kind'. It is broadly speaking the sciences which rely on observation which make prophecies, while those that rely principally on experiment make these technological predictions.

Historicists, for reasons which are explained in *The Poverty of Historicism*, tend to believe that sociological experiments are impractical and so the main task of the social sciences is prediction. The historicist thus tends to the notion that the task of the social sciences is similar to astronomy, namely to discover what the laws are and thus to make historical prophecies. Popper believes, on the contrary, that sociological experiment is not only possible but is all the time being carried out, that social science is more akin to physics. The setting up of the National Health Service, the launching of a new kind of insurance policy, even the opening of a hyper-market, are all sociological experiments. The conditions are less easy to control than they are in a physics laboratory; but even in a laboratory control is not by any means complete. Social scientists should be looking for laws, Popper thinks, analogous with physical laws, which forbid things, show what is impossible. The second law of thermo-dynamics in effect says 'You cannot build a machine which is 100 per cent efficient'. Analogous laws of social science might be, he suggests, 'You cannot have a full employment policy without in-flation', and 'You cannot, without increasing productivity, raise the real income of the working population', and thirdly 'You cannot equalise real incomes and at the same time raise productivity' (C.R., 343). Have these 'laws' been disproved? It would be nice to know whether we have been trying to lift ourselves by our own bootlaces.

Quite apart from its influence on Marxists, who espouse it openly, historicism exerts an unconscious influence on people of many different political persuasions who do not acknowledge the assumptions they are making. It is one of the great unconscious philosophies alluded to in Chapter 1. It is the source of the feeling that people have that 'we must move with the times' and 'keep up to date', that such and such 'is not good enough for the 1970s, and that we must 'prepare for the 1980s', etc. Above all it inspires the use of the word 'modern' in such a way as to extol uncritically whatever is being advocated that is new and to disparage whatever is old, however satisfactory. Historicism is there in the background, all the time justifying change for change's sake: e.g. yards to metres (although metres are two centuries old), as opposed to change in order to remove injustice or inefficiency or because something better has been found. For example, the Portsmouth road scheme, mentioned earlier in this chapter, is being sold to councillors as one 'to take the city into the mid-1990s'. The implication is that it is not enough to cure the existing bottlenecks and provide adequately for today's traffic. We must plan on an altogether bigger scale for the traffic of fifteen years ahead, although nobody can say where the petrol will come from, and the only evidence we have is to the effect that there was already a slight reduction in traffic flows in the year preceding the recent sharp increase in petrol prices.

Historicism is a less explicit and less coherent doctrine than holism – so much so that Popper found it necessary first to build up a good case for it before demolishing it. His arguments against historicism are, as usual, numerous. Here I shall state just two of them. He shows that the course of history is closely associated with the growth of knowledge, and strongly influenced by just such ideas as historicism and even more obviously by inventions – by World 3 in general. Such ideas and inventions are inherently unpredictable. 'For he who could predict today by scientific means our discoveries of tomorrow could make them today; which would mean that there would be an end to the growth of knowledge' (O.K., 298).

Secondly, the concept of society as a 'whole', as something that can move as a whole, whose course can be charted, however attractive it may be, is untenable. To illustrate its absurdity, Popper quotes the American historian, Henry Adams, who seriously hoped to determine the course of history by fixing two points on its track – one in the thirteenth century and the other in his own lifetime – and 'with the help of these two points . . . to project lines forward and backward' (P.H., 114).

Those who try to defend the idea of society moving 'as a whole' tend to do so by pointing to unmistakable trends. But trends are not necessarily irreversible. In the 1960s there was a trend for brick houses to be replaced with concrete flats and for central heating systems to be powered by electricity, etc. It is not now difficult to imagine a contrary trend. Laws cannot be reversed. A law asserts that something is impossible.

Historicism is a powerful and pervasive doctrine largely because it is so deeply unconscious. We disparage something as being out of date with barely a thought as to the basis of our disparagement. Especially does this attitude show in the polarisation towards tradition. Some are instantly hostile to tradition, others want blindly to uphold it. Obviously the rational attitude is that traditions are good or bad according to whether their effects are beneficial or harmful, something that is totally apart from age. Democracy itself is under attack as being out of date, the implication being that its admitted shortcomings are to be ascribed to the fact that the origins of it are ancient. It should not need to be said that the age of an idea has nothing to do with its validity.

Herbert Marcuse, a Marxist philosopher who had a vogue with students in the late 1960s, attempted to take Popper to task on the subject of his rejection of historicism and to ridicule his way of proceeding: 'What a strange method: to build up a position really worth attacking and then to attack it! . . . against what is he arguing? Who has actually maintained what he is so effectively destroying?' The answer to the second question is nobody; but in asking this question Marcuse shows that he fails to grasp two points which, as we have seen, are to Popper the main justification of philosophy as a discipline. First, that philosophical arguments are not directed against people, but against statements, or theories, or other arguments. Although these have been proposed by people, they stand in their own right and are true or false regardless of the personality or character or reliability of their authors. They are World 3 objects. Secondly, that much of what we do is based on tacit assumptions, philosophical positions that we have adopted without actually stating them and certainly without criticising them. Marcuse does not seem to realise the power of an unformulated theory, or how the clear formulation of it may be the first step to its rebuttal, or even how ideas that seem sensible in our minds sometimes look silly when we try to state them clearly in words.

Another of Popper's critics is a romantic, Paul Feyerabend, who, in a book which in essence is an attack on rationalism, compares Popper unfavourably with John Stuart Mill. 'Popper's philosophy, which some people would like to lay on us as the one and only humanitarian rationalism in existence today is but a pale reflection of Mill . . . it is . . . élitist, and is quite devoid of the concern for individual happiness that is such a characteristic feature of Mill.'

Élitism I have mentioned above; and as to concern for

individual happiness, Popper answered that criticism thirty years before it was made in this passage, which deserves quotation in full:

> Of all political ideals, that of making the people happy is perhaps the most dangerous one. It leads invariably to the attempt to impose our scale of 'higher' values upon others, in order to make them realise what seems to us of greatest importance for their happiness; in order, as it were, to save their souls. It leads to Utopianism and Romanticism. We all feel certain that everybody would be happy in the beautiful, the perfect community of our dreams. And no doubt, there would be heaven on earth if we could all love one another. But . . . the attempt to make heaven on earth invariably produces hell. It leads to intolerance. It leads to religious laws, and to the saving of souls through the inquisition.

He believes that it is based on a complete misunderstanding of our moral duties:

> It is our duty to help those who need our help: but it cannot be our duty to make others happy, since this does not depend on us, and since it would only too often mean intruding on the privacy of those towards whom we have such amiable intentions. The political demand for piecemeal (as opposed to Utopian) methods corresponds to the decision that the fight against suffering must be considered a duty, while the right to care for the happiness of others might be considered a privilege confined to the close circle of their friends. In their case, we may perhaps have a certain right to try to impose our scale of values – our preferences regarding music, for example. This right of ours exists only if, and because, they can get rid of us; because friendships can be ended. But the use of political means for imposing our scale of values upon others is a very different matter. Pain, suffering, injustice, and their prevention, these are the eternal problems of public morals, the 'agenda' of public

policy (as Bentham would have said). The 'higher' values should very largely be considered as 'non-agenda' and should be left to the realm of laissez-faire. (O.S., ii, 237)

Disagreeing with the slogan of the utilitarians 'the greatest happiness for the greatest number', Popper suggests 'One should demand, more modestly, the least amount of suffering for all; and further, that unavoidable suffering – such as hunger in times of unavoidable shortage of food – should be distributed as equally as possible.'

He mentions elsewhere the extreme difficulty experienced by Christians over the centuries in following the famous injunction to 'love your enemies' ('especially if they happen to be atheists or heretics'!). Sympathising with this difficulty he updates (to use an expression which he might condemn as historicist) this commandment to: 'Help your enemies; assist those in distress, even if they hate you; but love only your friends' (O.S., ii, 237).

Romantics have always attacked rationalists and realists as being cold and calculating, and have shown comparatively little interest in whether what they say is true. Typically, from this point of view, Feyerabend in upholding Mill as against Popper makes no mention of the fact that Popper has completely refuted the doctrine of psychologism (see page 72) which formed a central part of Mill's philosophy. And although part of the continuing importance of *The Open Society* in our day is its demolition of Marxism as science, Popper goes out of his way on this point to agree with Marx against Mill.

Feyerabend, in disparaging Popper vis-à-vis Mill, accuses Popper and most of his followers of 'unrelenting puritanism'. I invite the reader to judge that charge even on the many quotations from Popper in this book. Is it not likely that the puritans were in the forefront of his mind as an awful lesson when he wrote the passage just quoted about heaven or hell on earth? Feyerabend's disparagement amounts to little more than name-calling, the last resort of those whose arguments do not stand up.

The sociology of knowledge

The principal current opposition to the attitude of reasonableness rests on what is called the sociology of knowledge. This is the idea that truth is relative, that what is true for one historical period or social class is not necessarily true for another. It leads to such absurdities as there being things called proletarian science, bourgeois logic, and Jewish physics.

Here are two examples from current politics, one left and one right, of the depreciating effect of these ideas upon standards of truth and matters of fact. In their report on productivity in car factories, the Central Policy Review Staff (Think Tank) compared, among other things, the number of car doors turned out per hour by means of identical machinery in Ford's factories at Dagenham and at Genk in Belgium – 110 at Dagenham and 240 at Genk. *Sunday Times* reporters who visited the two factories and interviewed managers and workers, broadly confirmed these figures. But Mr Jack Jones, then General Secretary of the Transport and General Workers' Union, was concerned only to attack the report rather than to investigate the truth of it and the reasons behind the disparity. One of his associates summed up his attitude, saying 'The Think Tank report? It was an attack on the British working man, wasn't it?' One is reminded of the old joke about the smoker who was so shocked by what he read about the dangers of smoking that he gave up reading.

On the other side, the Conservative council who have landed themselves in an absurd road-planning muddle described on page 99 discount the perfectly rational protests against the scheme because the most-organised protesters are known to be supporters of the Labour Party.

The idea underlying the relativity of truth is the misconception of scientific objectivity which I touched on on page 13. This is that the objectivity of science depends upon the freedom from bias of the scientist. In fact it depends upon its public nature. A paper in a scientific journal is a World 3 object. If other scientists find that they cannot reproduce the results described, they will write and say so. Perhaps the original author will reply that they have misunderstood him. The experiments must be performed like this and not like that. Ultimately, as the result of criticism and counter-criticism, a consensus will emerge. In the first place, the new theory proposed may well attract attention because of the reputation or character of its proposer; but in the end it will become accepted as part of science only if it has stood up to criticism, and because of this alone. 'The objectivity of science', says Popper, 'is not a matter of individual scientists but rather the social result of their mutual criticism, of the friendly-hostile division of labour among scientists, of their co-operation and also their competition.' He sums it up with the aphorism 'What the sociology of knowledge misses is nothing less than the sociology of knowledge itself' (P.H., 155). Objectivity depends on such *social* ideas as competition between individual scientists and schools of thought, the critical tradition, publication in competing journals and through competing publishers, discussion at congresses, and the power of the state in tolerating free discussion.

The sociology of knowledge belongs to a group of modern philosophies whose tendency, Popper points out, is to unveil our hidden motives (O.S., 215). It is associated in this respect with psychoanalysis, Marxism, and the philosophy of meaning. They are popular for the reasons given on page 18. It is such fun to see through the follies of the unenlightened. They are very harmful because they destroy the intellectual basis of any discussion by establishing what he calls a reinforced dogmatism, because any attack against them rebounds on the attacker and shows him as a victim of his own complexes, social bias, meaningless ideas, etc. These philosophies are death to the ethic of reasonableness.

To summarise: rationalism cannot be proved; it is a kind of faith. The main ideas that are implied and embraced by it are the concept of truth as an absolute standard; the importance of language as communication and as clear expression of meaning rather than as means of clouding issues, and of discussion and criticism as means for the advance towards truth and as the only alternative to violence; and the belief in the unity of mankind in the sense that all men have something to contribute to human knowledge and to the general well-being, and that there is no natural barrier against co-operation and friendship.

4

Democracy in theory

The Open Society and its Enemies is the story of democracy, with an exhaustive explanation and reasoned advocacy of it, not as the best of all possible worlds, but as the best practical scheme so far invented, and one which is capable of almost indefinite improvement. Popper does not dodge the question: what is democracy? 'We may distinguish two main types of government. The first type consists of governments of which we can get rid without bloodshed; that is to say the social institutions provide means by which the rulers may be dismissed by the ruled, and the social traditions ensure that these institutions will not easily be destroyed by those who are in power. The second type consists of governments which the ruled cannot get rid of except by way of a successful revolution – that is to say, in most cases, not at all. I suggest the term "democracy" as a shorthand label for a government of the first type, and the term "tyranny" or "dictatorship" for the second.' And then, very characteristically, he adds 'and should anybody reverse this usage (as is frequently done nowadays), then I should simply say that I am in favour of what he calls tyranny' (O.S., i, 124). For Popper is impatient with those modern philosphers who see their task as being to find out what words or statements 'really mean'. (A witty spoof of this kind of philosophy appeared in the *Guardian*'s 1978 April-fool edition of *The Times* which reported that:

> a team of philosophers at Oxford has discovered a new meaning of the word 'and'. This brings to 18 the number of meanings found since the project began in the 1930s and puts the philosophers ahead in the competition with Cambridge scientists who are discovering sub-atomic particles.

Popper's method is to identify the realities he wants to talk about and give them suitable names. This involves pointing out that other philosophers and common usage have sometimes given the same name to different realities, with obvious confusion. Definitions, Popper says, should be read from right to left: 'democracy is a system where the government can be dismissed by the people' is better stated as 'a system where the people can dismiss the government is called democracy'.

Throughout history men have asked the question 'what is?', wanting to know the 'essential nature of'. Popper points out that this has on the whole been an unproductive question. It is usually not possible to find a satisfactory answer. It was only when essentialism was abandoned in favour of nominalism that science began to advance. This term means giving names to things but has come to mean asking the question: how does it behave, what are its properties and characteristics? We still do not have satisfactory answers to the questions about the essential nature of light, matter, atoms, electricity, etc., but we nevertheless have a wealth of knowledge about them and how they behave.

Popper's definition of democracy may seem bare and inadequate; but he points out that in no conceivable system can you or I rule. In no conceivable way can the differing ideas of sixty million people be combined in, say, British foreign policy. The essential point is that in some general way the rulers are controlled by the ruled, even if it amounts to no more than that they can be dismissed. (I shall suggest in Chapter 11 how it may be possible to achieve a 'plastic' control without necessarily going to the length of dismissal or the threat of it.)

Popper's philosophy of politics diverges from that of Plato (and so much in modern politics that can be traced back to Plato) in that he rejects the question that was paramount in Plato's eyes, the question 'who should rule?'. To Popper this is a red herring. The really important question is how the rulers, whoever they are, can be *controlled*. He elaborates this as 'How can we so organise

political institutions that even bad or incompetent rulers can
be prevented from doing too much damage?'

Who should rule would indeed be the vital question if
the theory of unchecked sovereignty were true, that is if it
were true that whoever has the power can do as he likes.
This theory is in fact taken for granted by those who in
modern times think the important question is who should
dictate, the capitalists or the workers. But Popper points
out that no political power is ever unchecked. 'Even the
most powerful tyrant depends upon his secret police, his
henchmen, his hangman.' He is forced to play one group
off against another.

The open society

Popper's theory of historical development is based on the
idea of two extreme forms of society – closed and open. In
their pure form both may be theoretical abstracts. A society
completely closed in his sense may never have existed.
Certainly no completely open one has. But direction and
change towards or away from greater openness is easily
detectable.

The closed society is the typical tribal society in which
each man has a fixed place and role and where there is no
provision for a change of status. 'Taboos rigidly regulate
and dominate all aspects of life. They do not leave many
loop-holes. There are few problems in this form of life,
nothing really equivalent to moral problems. I do not
mean to say that a member of a tribe does not sometimes
need much heroism and endurance in order to act in
accordance with the taboos. What I mean is that he may
rarely find himself in the position of doubting how he
ought to act.' In the open society on the other hand there
is constant changing of social position: 'Many members
strive to rise socially, and to take the places of other
members. This may lead, for example, to such important
social phenomena as class struggle' (O.S., i, 101). Taboos
remain and all known societies have a certain rigidity of
class structure. But there has been a fitful, irregular, and

often temporarily reversed movement away from the completely closed society in the direction of greater openness at any rate since the Athens of the sixth and fifth centuries B.C. Popper thinks that the beginning of seafaring and commerce, both of which demand some individual initiative, were the start of the movement helped on by the beginning, for whatever reason, of criticism, of the idea that doctrines and taboos and customs and 'knowledge' might be looked at objectively and criticised.

Roberts, in his history already quoted, points to the special historical importance of the Hebrew prophets. Until their time, might was right. The king was the law. Their great innovation was the idea of an absolute standard by which even the king might be judged.

> It is not too much to say that, if the heart of political
> liberalism is the belief that power must be used within a
> moral framework independent of it, then its tap root is
> the teaching of the prophets.

This was a vital step in the development of those institutions and traditions which, in Popper's definition of democracy, enable the ruled to rid themselves on occasions of the rulers.

The breakdown of the closed society in Athens led quickly to the rise of democracy in the age of Pericles; but it was short-lived. One of the most influential contributors to its fall was the great philospher Plato. The first volume of *The Open Society* is devoted to an analysis of Plato's political thought and the way in which it has led to confusion down to the present time by its apparent concern with freedom and justice while advocating a totalitarian regime. One vital issue which Plato succeeded in confusing for all future generations was that of individualism. This word, Popper points out, has two distinct meanings; the opposite of collectivism and the opposite of altruism, unselfishness, public-spiritedness. Plato ignored the first sense and managed to convince his contemporaries and posterity that individualists were necessarily selfish egoists and that the only alternative to selfishness is collectivism, that there is no such thing as the unselfish altruistic individualist. Popper unmasks this deception and points to Charles Dickens as a perfect example of this supposedly non-existent type. 'It would be difficult to say', he wrote, 'which is the stronger, his [Dickens's] passionate hatred of selfishness or his passionate interest in individuals with all their human weaknesses; and this attitude is combined with a dislike not only of . . . collectives, but even of a genuinely devoted altruism, if directed towards anonymous groups rather than concrete individuals (c.f. Mrs Jellyby in Bleak House "a lady devoted to public duties")' (O.S., i, 101). Plato attacked individualism, Popper believes, because he recognised that, even more than equalitarianism, it was such a power in the new humanitarian creed.

> The emancipation of the individual was indeed the great spiritual revolution which had led to the breakdown of tribalism and to the rise of democracy . . . This individualism, united with altruism, has become the basis of our western civilisation. It is the central doctrine of Christianity ('Love your neighbour', say the scriptures, not 'love your tribe') and it is the core of all ethical doctrines which have grown from our civilisation and stimulated it.

Compare also Kant's saying 'Always recognise that human individuals are ends, and do not use them as mere means to your ends.' 'There is no other thought', says Popper, 'which has been so powerful in the moral development of man' (O.S., i, 102).

His idea of historical development as a general trend from the closed society towards the open one may at first sight look like historicism, the very idea he most consistently attacks. But Popper does not say that history inevitably moves in a steady progression onward from the closed society. On the contrary history records many reversals – the dark ages, the Fascist domination of Europe in the 1930s and '40s, and of South America and South Africa now. The opening of human society is something that has happened. He hopes it will go on. He thinks we should encourage it; but its advance is not inevitable although it *is* linked with the growth of knowledge, which is also capable of being halted and reversed.

Throughout the ages writers have invoked the organic theory of society, they have likened human societies to living organisms, drawing an analogy between the members of a tribe or nation and the members or limbs or organs of the body. Popper concedes that in the closed society there is some justification for this analogy but from the moment that a society begins to 'open' the analogy breaks down completely. For there is nothing in the individual organism remotely corresponding to, for instance, the class struggle. There is no kind of tendency for a leg to become an arm or a heart to take the place of a brain. John Donne's well known sermon describes an attribute of the closed society, for although it may be true that 'no man is an island', it is palpably untrue in a society even as open as ours that 'The bell' always 'tolls for thee'. Far from losing by the death of others, individuals in our society frequently profit both materially and psychologically and are in no sense diminished. The closed society is like an organism in the sense that it is united by physical factors of bodily contact and direct personal relationships; the open society is characterised by a degree of abstractness. The abstract society is an unrealisable imaginary society outlined by Popper to illustrate an extreme. In it individuals never actually meet in the flesh but interact by letter, telephone, bill, cheque (and even artificial insemination!).

The increasing abstraction of the open society is one of the factors leading to what is called the strain of civilisation. It is created by the effort which life in a partially open and abstract society demands from us and is felt most in times of rapid social change. It arises from 'the endeavour to be rational, to forgo at least some of our emotional social needs, to look after ourselves, and to accept responsibilities. We must, I believe, bear this strain as the price to be paid for every increase in knowledge, in reasonableness, in cooperation and in mutual help, and consequently in our chances of survival'. It is of the same nature as the strain felt by the child on leaving the shelter of the parental home.

> There is no return to a harmonious state of nature. If we turn back, then we must go the whole way, we must return to the beasts. If we wish to remain human, then there is only one way, the way into the open society. We must go on into the unknown, the uncertain and insecure, using what reason we may have to plan as well as we can for both security *and* freedom (O.S., i, 201).

The state

Karl Marx defined the state as 'an organ of class discrimination, an organ for the oppression of one class by another; its aim is the creation of an "order" which legalises and perpetuates this oppression'. For Popper the state is a society for the prevention of crime, its essential function being the protection of the meek and weak in both the physical and the economic sense. It is an organisation for the restraint of physical and economic bullying.

Marx gave an appalling account of the working conditions of his time. Popper quotes from *Das Kapital* a number of examples of children working a fifteen-hour day from the age of under seven and of young women working even longer, in some cases to their death. 'Using the slogan "equal and free competition for all" ', Popper commented, 'the unrestrained capitalism of this period resisted successfully all labour legislation until 1833, and its practical execution for many years more. The consequence was a life of desolation and misery which can hardly be imagined in our day.'

> Marx's burning protest against these crimes, which were than tolerated, not only by professional economists but also by churchmen, will secure him forever a place among the liberators of mankind . . . .

I believe that the injustice and inhumanity of the unrestrained 'capitalist system' described by Marx cannot be questioned, but it can be interpreted in terms of . . . the paradox of freedom. Freedom defeats itself if it is unlimited. Unlimited freedom means that a strong man is free to bully a weak one and to rob him of his freedom. This is why we demand that the state should limit freedom to a certain extent, so that everybody's freedom is protected by the law. Nobody should be at the *mercy* of others but all should have the right to be protected by the state (O.S., ii, 124).

He quotes with approval the apocryphal story of the judge who told the accused 'Your freedom to swing your fist is limited by the proximity of your neighbour's jaw'. In the same vein is the comment on her adopted country by a G.I. bride after twenty-five years in the United States: 'This is a country where they scream freedom from the roof tops; but what's the use of freedom when you're afraid to go out at night?'

The formal or legal freedom, despised by Marx, the right of the people to choose and dismiss their government, is the only known device by which we can try to protect ourselves against the misuse of political power. It is the ultimate control of the rulers by the ruled. And since political power can control economic power (see below), political democracy is the only means for the control of economic power by the ruled. Without democratic control there is no earthly reason why a government should not use its power for purposes very different from the protection of the freedom of its citizens. The remedy against economic exploitation and injustice 'must be a political remedy similar to the one we use against physical violence'.

Economic power

Marx, misled by the power in his day of the capitalist over the workers, thought that economic power is necessarily superior to political power. Politics, he wrote, could do no more than 'shorten the birth pangs' of the inevitable revolution. Hence the need for the state to own the means of production, distribution etc., and hence the British Labour Party's belief in the need to own 'the commanding heights of the economy'. The argument, roughly, was that he who has the money has the power because if necessary he can buy guns to enforce his power. But, Popper argues, this is only the first stage. Those that have the guns can see this too; and so you may end up by having both the money and the guns in the same hands. Marx failed to see that even in his own day the capitalists owed their power of exploitation to the political power of the state which legalised their profits and protected them against personal violence and theft. Bertrand Russell (1938) gave two historical examples to demonstrate that political power was necessarily superior to the power of money.

> Julius Caesar was helped to power by his creditors who saw no hope of repayment except through his success; but when he had succeeded he was powerful enough to defy them. Charles V borrowed money from the Fuggers in order to buy the position of emperor; but when he became emperor he snapped his fingers at them and they lost what they had lent.

The pre-occupation of the British Left with ownership has had two unfortunate consequences. Firstly there has been this tendency to blame people – capitalists, managers etc. – and thus to imply that all that is needed is to hand over the running of things to new managers with the right (i.e. Left) ideas. Disillusionment sets in when the ownership is changed and the management given to people of socialist sympathies and the result is not only a service or industry that loses money, but one that shows even less signs than the privately-owned one of being run in the interests of its customers. Probably no private company would have dared to treat its customers as cavalierly as did the publicly-owned electricity supply industry. Having induced people to invest in electric appliances for space and water heating by offering attractive off-peak discounts, they then proceeded to cut the discount very substantially.

Secondly, the obsession with ownership and the political attitude of management has diverted thought from the important consideration of how an industry should be run and what its priorities should be. It is typical of the muddle over public ownership that the Labour government's own *Transport Policy* white paper should insist on the need to preserve competition between three nationally-owned industries – rail, air, and bus – on the inter-city passenger services, when part of the rationale for public ownership was the elimination of wasteful competition.

In Shaw's play *The Apple Cart*, any invention to make a commodity more durable was immediately bought up and suppressed by the powerful monopoly, Breakages Ltd. British Rail's research engineers have come up with an ingeniously simple solution (which G. Freeman Allen described) to the important problem of transferring goods cheaply and safely from road to rail and back to road. This has been suppressed, according to Joseph Hanlon, as effectively as if Breakages had been involved, by the bureaucratic, inverted Heller, technique of estimating (or rather over-estimating) the costs of development.

On the whole the theory prevailing, though not often spelt out, in the Labour Party (an organisation now somewhat averse to theorising) is what Popper called a Vulgar Marxist Conspiracy Theory (O.S., ii, 101), in which the exploitation of workers is seen as a malevolent conspiracy by capitalists. This theory, Popper pointed out, has largely replaced in both overt and quasi Marxist circles the 'ingenious and highly original' doctrine of Marx himself that capitalists as much as workers were helpless puppets pulled by economic wires, helpless victims of historical forces.

An extraordinary apparent contradiction between fact and theory faced both Marxists and quasi Marxists when early in 1979 the workers who went on strike against low wages were not the exploited employees of capitalist industry but their less well-off brothers in the public services. *Their* bosses could not possibly be seen as grinding their faces for the sake of profits. Their bosses' only purpose was to provide services for a public which included those worse off than the strikers; and the former were certainly the ones that suffered most.

Interventionism

Marx took the appalling conditions of early industrial life as being an essential part of capitalism and predicted that inevitably they would get worse. It is one of many of his prophecies which did not come true. It would have been true of unrestrained, laissez-faire, capitalism, Popper believes; but even while Marx was writing, partly as a result of his writing, the restraint of capitalism was beginning. The conditions he so vividly described have everywhere ceased to exist. Economic interventionism has everywhere been adopted, and this has undoubtedly resulted in an enormous improvement in working conditions and in living standards too.

Economic interventionism has had two arrows to its bow. The first was legal – the British Factory Acts, limiting by law the hours of labour and the age of the employed, were the first restraint. Later followed the trade unions, which gave the employed the means of bargaining with the employers. 'Workers of the world unite; you have nothing to lose but your chains' was a piece of advice that was taken and a prophecy that did come true. They did unite and did lose their chains – and not much else.

Revolution and peaceful change

Marxism and other revolutionary theories, Popper pointed out, suffer in a democracy from an inner contradiction at least as fundamental as that which Marx attributed to capitalism. It is this: in order to attract sufficient support revolutionaries must campaign for the improvement of the conditions of the workers that they wish to recruit. But what if their campaign succeeds? If wages rise and conditions generally improve, they must say it is not enough. They must demand more. But with each improvement fewer and fewer workers are dissatisfied with the status quo. The revolutionaries are thus 'forced to fight for the immediate betterment of the workers' lot, but to hope at the same time for the opposite'. The contradiction produces a stage in which 'it is hard to know who is the traitor, since treachery may be faithfulness and faithfulness treachery'. Popper wrote this during the war but it is still very much to the point. The British Left is still very much divided between those who want to do something 'within the system' and those who want to destroy the system and are therefore forced to be two-faced. They have to advocate better conditions without really wanting their advocacy to succeed.

The difference between the views of Marx and Popper in regard to the nature or function of the state draws attention to the ambivalent way in which we now regard the chief agent of the internal power of the state – the police. Popper regards the police as the most important element in the maintenance of freedom. They are the means by which the law is enforced; and freedom from every kind of bullying and exploitation ultimately rests on their ability to uphold the law. This view has nothing to do of course with the moral character of individual policemen nor whether there is widespread corruption in any particular police force. A police force is essential, just as a government is essential. Popper's interest in the police as such is the same as his interest in all other political institutions: how can we so organise the police that even bad policemen cannot do too much damage? It seems to me that one of the things we might do is to relieve them as far as possible of their function as enforcers of what may be unpopular government or local government policy and so let them concentrate on being the protectors of the public. I have in mind the setting up of more separate forces like the customs officers and the traffic wardens, distinct from the police, to take over such things as the activities of the drug squads.

There is an asymmetry in this matter of law and its

enforcement which is somewhat analogous to the asymmetry between the possibility of refuting a theory and the impossibility of confirming it. Changes in the law must be made by democratic discussion and not by force; but once the change is made it must be maintained by force. One can think of it as a kind of ratchet mechanism, the discussion and democratic decision being the winding up, while the police are the pawl that prevents slipping back to lawlessness.

Two kinds of intervention

The state must intervene to prevent physical and economic bullying; but Popper makes an important but little recognized distinction between 'two entirely different methods by which the intervention of the state may proceed. The first is that of designing a legal framework of protective institutions. ... The second is that of empowering organs of the state to act ... as they consider necessary for achieving the ends laid down by the rulers' (O.S., ii, 131-3).

At first sight one might imagine that the second method of leaving a matter to the discretion of a committee or official would be less restricting than laying down a definite law; and it does seem that this is often assumed to be the case.

The operation of the fire precaution laws is the example of this difference of method which first comes to my mind. The first method would be to lay down by law that, for example, all buildings of more than three storeys must have an external fire-resistant escape stairway. This might prove unnecessary or impossibly costly, in which case the law would be amended to require this only in certain specified circumstances. What we have in fact is that, if such a building is occupied by more than one household (one household can burn so far as the law is concerned), then means of escape must be provided 'to the satisfaction' of some authority who may be the fire officer. This is the second method. Now this kind of arrangement is open to all kinds of abuse and can even make life more dangerous for the people it is supposed to protect.

Here are two instances known to me. In one case a couple, who let their second-floor rooms to summer holiday-makers, were told that they must do some £1,500 worth of fire-precaution work. They were *not* told that, if they ceased to let rooms, they need not make any changes at all, as they would be a single household. In another case an eighty-year-old widow who lived alone upstairs in her four-storey house, but had a young couple living in her semi-basement, was told that she must evict them. She was thereby condemned to live entirely alone and was deprived, in the event of fire, of the help of an able-bodied couple. Had there been a steel fire escape from her top storey where nobody slept, she would have been allowed to keep her basement tenants – a slight case of tunnel-vision!

The lack of a definite standard that can be disputed has meant that architects have to play safe. You cannot wait until you have erected an expensive building and then find that the fire officer will not approve it. You put in double the number of fire doors that he could conceivably demand; and you put springs on them so strong that elderly people cannot open them. (They then have to be propped open and so lose all purpose.) While the main staircase used to be the central feature of many public buildings, play-safe architects now have often to hide it away and box it in behind spring-loaded doors. There would be something to be said for the system if it really saved lives. But the fact is that the four fires that have cost the most lives in the past decade have all been in new buildings which must have been passed by the fire officers. Lord James of Rusholme, chairman of the Royal Fine Art Commission, in a letter to *The Times* (8 September 1978) protesting about the aesthetic damage being done by over-enthusiastic fire precautions, said that in 'the many historic buildings of the University of Oxford . . . only one death by fire appears to have been recorded in the last 400 years'. He added that 'the risk taken by the public in using such buildings is . . . negligible when compared with the risk taken on the roads to get *to* them'.

In the case of the first method (of state intervention), Popper says: 'The legal framework can be known and understood by the individual citizen . . . Its function is predictable. It introduces a feature of certainty and security into social life. When it is altered, allowances can be made, during a transitional period, for those individuals who have laid their plans in the expectation of its constancy.' The other method (personal intervention by civil servants etc.), he says, 'must introduce an ever-growing element of unpredictability into social life, and with it will develop the feeling that social life is irrational and insecure. The use of discretionary powers is liable to grow quickly, once it has become an accepted method, since adjustments will be necessary, and adjustments to discretionary short-term decisions can hardly be carried out by institutional means'. The tendency, he says, must create 'the impression that there are hidden powers behind the scenes, making people susceptible to the conspiracy theory of society with all its consequences – heresy hunts, national, social, and class hostility.'

It seems to me likely that the growing tendency to govern by these discretionary powers is a major cause of discontent and of the widespread feeling that democracy is a sham. Whichever party is in power, 'they' will carry on regardless. Popper himself gives several reasons why governments and civil servants tend to adopt the discretionary method; but, he says:

The most important reason is undoubtedly that the significance of the distinction between the two methods is not understood. The way to its understanding is blocked to the followers of Plato, Hegel, and Marx. They will never see that the old question 'Who shall be the rulers?' must be superseded by the more real one 'How shall we tame them?' (O.S., ii, 133).

Democracy and induction connected

To return to the essential point of democracy: the control of the rulers by the ruled must depend on a two-way exchange of information. The rulers must know what the people want and what is the effect of their ruling, and the people must know what the rulers are trying to do and why. The rulers are bound to make mistakes; and rational government can be carried out only if it is subject to criticism so that the mistakes can be pointed out and the lessons learnt.

There is an obvious parallel between the above paragraph and the concluding paragraph of Chapter 1, where it was emphasised that science depends on communication between scientists and potential critics.

We are now in a position to appreciate the far-reaching importance, already mentioned, of the fact that induction is not a valid method and of Popper's solution of the resulting problem, his demonstration that science, and action generally, can nevertheless be rational. If induction were the source of knowledge and if a theory could be corroborated by finding confirmations of it (white swans), then scientists working alone or in groups, committees of experts etc., could be left on their own to arrive at the truth or the next best thing. But the fact that induction is not valid and that truth emerges as a result of criticism – of attempts to refute theories (to find black swans) – means that critics, who may well be people who know far less than the experts, are necessary to the process. For no man can be relied on to criticise sufficiently searchingly his own ideas; and no planner can know all the implications of his own plans.

In the political and social fields there has been an attempt to emulate the success of the physical sciences by taking over their machinery. Computers, statistical methods, decision-theory – these it is sometimes thought, will give to political decisions the validity that they seem to have given to scientific results. The idea arises from a misunderstanding of science. These things are the trappings, the apparatus, of science. The validity of the results depends, as we have seen, on their public-ness, on the fact that anybody with the necessary skill can repeat the experiments and calculations for himself and point out any mistakes.

This is the connection between science and democracy.

This is why each depends on the other. Technology can flourish in secrecy and under tyrannical regimes, but new knowledge depends upon open-ness and on public criticism for its validity. Politicians and planners can use their expertise to work out anything from the rebuilding of a city to a new pension scheme, but they will not see all the snags without the aid of the people affected.

This is perhaps the most important of all the conclusions that arise from Popper's work; the fact that experts and specialists of all kinds from physicists to civil servants are not sufficient unto themselves, cannot find out the truth or lay down the law by themselves, but depend on the public at large in order to substantiate the truth and the validity of what they do, although even then there is no certainty. This is the case for democracy.

5

Psychology against culture

In the introduction to this book I quoted from J. M. Roberts's *History* that 'The message men took from Freud ... called in question the very foundation of liberal civilization itself, the idea of the rational, responsible, consciously-motivated individual.' 'Freud's importance beyond science lay in providing a new mythology', Roberts writes, and he adds 'It was to prove highly corrosive.' On behaviourism, the mechanistic psychology that was founded on Pavlov's 'conditioning', Roberts says that 'the diffused effect ... seems curiously parallel to that of Freudianism, in that its bias is towards the demolition of the sense of responsibility and individualism which is the heart of the European and Christian tradition'.

This cultural tradition is based above all things on the idea of truth, that is on correspondence with the facts. This is in strong contrast with most Eastern philosophies. Anybody who has travelled in the East knows how the most respectable Asiatic will, if disposed to please, answer a question, not primarily on the basis of fact, but rather on what he hopes will please the questioner. Science, based on the idea of theories which correspond with the facts, is essentially a Western invention. It never could have arisen in the East. Now, paradoxically, two Western psychologies have undermined the concept of truth with their own science, the one with a general blurring of distinctions and the other by reducing truth to the answer we are programmed to give. They have knocked away their own foundation.

However if either were to stand up to attempts to refute it we should have to accept it as provisionally established no matter what its effect. But I shall maintain that both are myths. While the Freudian theories are unfalsifiable and therefore metaphysical, I shall attempt to show in the next chapter that conditioning can be logically disproved.

I shall devote most of this chapter to the 'corrosive' effect, particularly of the Freudian outlook, although, as Roberts has implied, much that can be said against one applies also to the other. First I shall show how psychology as a subject, independently of its authorship, has tended to assume an exaggerated importance (a) because of the omission of World 3 (under whatever name) from the scheme of things and (b) because of the false doctrine of 'psychologism'.

We have been too much concerned with unconscious motivation rather than with conscious intentions, purposes, and interests; too much concerned with what we have in common with other animals rather than with what makes us unique. And even those who are concerned exclusively with human studies seem often to miss the point. Here, for example, is an excerpt from the introduction to a book called *Human Behaviour* by Claire and W. M. S. Russell. 'What makes us human', they say, 'is our capacity for furthering each other's explorations by a process of creative communication between us. Our enquiry will therefore have two closely related phases or departments, the study of individual behaviour, and that of the relations between individuals – the study of social relations.' This hardly exhausts the range of human life, in fact it does not seem to make us very different from bees – just that our communications are capable of greater precision. It virtually excludes from consideration the world of abstractions. Popper's World 3, the world of the products of the human mind, theories, myths, designs, etc., which exist independently of their creators but react on us all.

A very large part of our waking lives is spent in such 'behaviour' as talking about non-material things, ideas, intentions etc., reading, writing, calculating, making things to a design, cooking to a recipe, operating machinery, following a map, time-table, or other technical reference, looking at pictures; and we even think about and are influenced by what happened before we were born, and we make plans for or dream dreams about a far off future.

Although all this could be called 'individual behaviour' it is very different from what is called animal behaviour and nothing to do with social relations.

What makes us human is our capacity to interact not only with each other but with the world of abstractions and ideas, with World 3. This is what is absolutely unique about us. It depends upon human language and it leads, as Popper has pointed out, to a greater importance in our lives of control from above, of conscious intention over unconscious 'animal' motivation. An entry in an engagement diary may be the prime cause of the movement of the physical body of a man across the Atlantic ('Compton's problem') and that engagement may be kept in spite of an unconscious reluctance to keep it. An attitude of aggressive hostility can be transformed at once into one of cooperation when, for example, one grasps a new explanation of someone else's behaviour.

It is important to note that this interaction with World 3 is not confined to intellectuals or even to literates. All who use human language are constantly interacting with objective ideas such as age, death, good value, fairness, next year, laws and rules, and with theories even if they are false, mere superstitions, or old wives' tales. Popper's example, quoted in Chapter 2, about the practical difference between thinking today is Saturday and saying today is Saturday, makes the point. The second can be criticised, the first cannot.

The capacity for interaction between individual minds and the products both of our own minds and those of others (living or dead) is the exclusively human achievement. Its existence and its central importance in our lives must make us profoundly suspicious of any attempts to deduce norms of human society from the behaviour of apes.

The exaggerated importance given in our time to psychology depends also on a doctrine which formed a central part of the philosophy of John Stuart Mill. Mill recognised that human behaviour is a consequence not only of human psychology but also of material and social institutions. We do what we do very largely because of material constraints imposed by our houses, roads, clothes etc., and also because of customs and laws and the institutions of family, commerce, employment and so on. But, Mill maintained, since all these things were human inventions, they were themselves ultimately reducible to human psychology. This reduction is what Popper calls 'psychologism' and he shows it to be false.

Much of what is written tends to play down even the part played by social institutions, whatever their origin, and assumes that psychology is the only factor. It is worth emphasising the importance of institutions and the comparative unimportance, in some situations, of psychology. The brief summary of the causes of the outbreak of the first world war at the beginning of Chapter 7 is a good example of this – how the war would most probably not have started, whatever the psychology of the statesmen concerned, had the war plans of the various great powers not existed, or had they been more flexible.

Popper's technique in demolishing psychologism, the doctrine that social laws must ultimately be reducible to psychological laws, is the same as with historicism: to make the best possible case for this view – better perhaps than most people who uncritically assume the truth of it could make – and then to refute it. In making the case for psychologism, one has first to admit that no action is ever explained by motives or any other psychological or behavioural concept alone. There is always the environment, the general situation, ranging from laws and customs to all kinds of physical restraints. (One walks along the road or footpath although the direct way to one's destination may be through someone else's house or garden.) But the case, then, for psychologism is, admitting the influence and restraint of the environment, that the *social* environment is man–made. Institutions, the market for example, are derived from human psychology which disposes towards the pursuit of wealth: and the fact that human life is so much a matter of institutions is itself due to a peculiarity of human psychology. Furthermore the origins of all the institutions that now govern human society must be explicable in terms of human psychology since at some stage in history they have been introduced for some human purpose. Thus, to quote Mill: 'All phenomena of society are phenomena of human nature and the laws of the phenomena of society are, and can be, nothing but the laws of the actions and passions of human beings, that is to say, the laws of individual human nature.'

This is an impressive argument; but more impressive to me is the way in which Popper demolishes it.

> If all regularities in social life, the laws of our social environment, of all institutions etc., are ultimately explained by, and reduced to, the 'actions and passions of human beings' then such an approach forces upon us not only the idea of historico–causal development, but also the idea of the *first steps* of such a development. For the stress on the psychological origin of social rules or institutions can only mean that they can be traced back to a state when their introduction was dependent solely upon psychological factors, or more precisely, when it was independent of any established social institutions.

Psychologism was thus forced, whether it liked it or not, Popper showed, to operate with the idea of a *beginning* of society and with the idea of a human nature and a human psychology as they existed prior to society:

> It is a desperate position . . . This theory of a pre-social human nature which explains the foundation of society is not only an historical myth, but also, as it were, a methodological myth. (O.S. 92–3)

As Popper says, it can hardly be seriously discussed because we have every reason to believe that man's immediate ancestors were social. Thus social institutions and sociological laws must have existed before 'what some people are pleased to call "human nature" ' and before human psychology. Thus sociology is prior to psychology and if a reduction is to be made at all, it would be more hopeful to attempt a reduction of psychology to sociology than the other way round.

As usual Popper has several arguments to pile on top of this one; but this is the most easily understood and is sufficient by itself. It always reminds me, in its elegance, of the proof, also a *reductio ad absurdum*, attributed to Pythagoras of the irrationality of the square root of two. (Nothing to do, of course with unreasonableness. An irrational number is one that cannot be expressed as the *ratio* of two whole numbers.) Another way of saying the same thing is to say that it is impossible to measure the diagonal of a square whose side is one unit. At first sight, as in the present case, one would not imagine it possible to prove such a proposition by mere logic applied to undisputed facts. The importance of proving the (psychologism) case is directly related to the fact that the opposite is widely assumed. Freud, for example, according to his biographer Ernest Jones, said that sociology 'can be nothing other than applied psychology'.

Popper uses competition as an example of a social phenomenon which cannot be attributed to psychology. It is after all usually undesired by the competitors themselves and 'must be explained as a (usually inevitable) unintended consequence of (conscious and planned) actions of the competitors'. Competition to purchase a house, used in Chapter 1 as an example against the conspiracy theory, is a case in point. 'Thus', says Popper, 'even though we may be able to explain psychologically some of the actions of the competitors, the social phenomenon of competition is a psychologically inexplicable consequence of these actions.' ('The logic of the Social Sciences'.) The popularity of such assumptions as the conspiracy theory underlines the importance of the refutation of psychologism. Conspiracy theory irrationally explains adverse events psychologically in terms of individual motives, thus encouraging groundless enmity and disaffection. It is like blaming the government for the weather.

I return now to the cultural impact of modern psychology. 'Psychologists say', we read frequently in the newspapers by way of introduction to some highly questionable piece of dogma; but, in fact, as David Cohen's interesting collection of interviews shows, his selection of the world's best-known psychologists are agreed on practically nothing. Nevertheless, however much they disagree in detail, the diffused effect, to use Roberts's expression, of their studies is an atmosphere of determinism and therefore of irresponsibility. However successful the Freudian and behaviourist theories have been within, so to speak, their own terms of reference, their cultural influence, pervasive, excessive, has been on the whole vicious and tending to run counter to all that I have subsumed under the term rationalism, as well as being very largely against common sense. It is necessary to qualify this statement with the phrase 'on the whole' because one cannot deny that, for example, the amelioration of the often harsh conditions for children in institutions of all sorts owes a lot to Freud's interest in children's mental processes. And there have been other benefits – a relaxation of puritanical standards, but these of course have been relaxed at other times in history without the aid of this particular psychology.

In a recent four-page article on Freud, covering the various revisions and heresies of Freudianism and its offshoots and sects, Laurie Taylor, a professor of sociology, did not once pose the question to what extent any of the theories he mentioned was true; and he ended it by quoting from another journal: 'with Copernicus the earth moved from its position of centrality in the universe, with Darwin man moved from his position of centrality in the eye of the creator, with Marx the individual human subject moved from its position of centrality in history, and with Freud consciousness moved from its position of centrality in the structure of the psyche.' The professor's comment was that this provides an explanation of Freud's enduring significance for social scientists. But there is another way of looking at the significance of these great thinkers.

Popper and his co-author Sir John Eccles gave as one of the reasons for writing their new book *The Self and its Brain* that 'the debunking of man has gone far enough –

even too far'. They refer to this same decentralising argument and then say 'but since Copernicus we have learnt to appreciate how wonderful and rare, perhaps even unique, our little earth is in this big universe; and since Darwin we have learned more about the incredible organisation of all living things on earth and also about the unique position of man among his fellow creatures' (S.B., VII). They might have added that since Freud began his decentralising of consciousness, and therefore of reason, the practical achievements of reason have been greater than in the whole of previous history. Computers, television, space travel, atomic energy, the incredibly detailed recent knowledge about, for example, ultra-microscopic biological structures and processes – you don't have to like all these things, but it cannot be denied that even if their inventors did labour under unresolved complexes and even if they were motivated by unconscious infantile fantasies, they achieved all this by science and reason.

An analytical theory, by postulating underlying elements in a whole, may help to explain observations; but it cannot alter them. What seems to me to be the mistake in analytical psychology can be illustrated by an analogy from physics. I know that the accepted theory is that this table I am writing on consists mostly of space in which electrons are revolving around nuclei. The theory explains the observed fact that the table can be sawn in half or converted into smoke and ashes; but it in no way detracts from the solidity of the table. I may lean on it as hard as if I had never heard of atoms. Psychoanalysis has tended to imply, in the terms of this analogy, 'It is not *really* solid. Do not treat it as a table, always remember it is really an assemblage of particles'. And in its own field what it is saying is 'People are not really people. They are assemblages of instincts and complexes masquerading as people'. Because it has analysed such qualities as loyalty, patriotism, public-spiritedness, and integrity, and found them to be derived from certain infantile impulses, it tends to imply that these qualities are therefore not what they seem. Its tendency is thus to disparage if not to discount all that we most value and admire in each other. It is a kind of not-seeing-the-wood-for-the-trees, a form of induction. It is a mistake that physics has never made.

The revolution that Freud initiated was a revolution against a two thousand-year-old European tradition that virtue was something to be inculcated, a morality to be taught directly or by example, and superimposed on an animal nature. Freudian analysis in contrast consisted of a systematic unpeeling of the encrustation of the culturally-acquired 'super-ego' to free the natural 'id' from which all goodness flowed. (I am referring here to the early, pre-first world war, phase of Freud's theorising, which was the source of Roberts's 'diffused effect', before the clarity was blurred by second thoughts, for example in *Civilization and Its Discontents*.) Modern biology has, I think, vindicated the traditional view. Nature *is*, in Tennyson's phrase, red in tooth and claw. This is the importance of Dawkins's *The Selfish Gene* from which I have already quoted. Dawkins exposes the error in the view, assumed by many distinguished biologists – Konrad Lorenz among them – that natural selection works to secure the interests of the species or some other group. Dawkins demonstrates that it must work at a lower level even than that of the individual. It works at the level of the gene. The self-sacrifice, apparently in the interests of the group, demonstrated for example by some members of insect colonies is in fact part of this blind process of short-term self-interest of the gene. (The self-sacrificing members are always the sterile ones. The genes in their bodies will not survive whatever they do.)

This self-interest of the gene is inherent in all living things; but it does not preclude a conscious far-seeing 'conspiracy of doves' (page 30). He coins the term *meme* to describe the elements in the uniquely human process of cultural evolution, elements of World 3 – ideas, snatches of a tune, slogans, etc., – which replicate themselves in a manner analogous to the self-replicating segments of DNA, the genes. 'We have at least the mental equipment', Dawkins says, 'to foster our long term selfish interests. . . . We can see the long-term benefits of participating in a "conspiracy of doves", and we can sit down together to discuss ways of making the conspiracy work. We have the power to defy the selfish genes of our birth and, if necessary, the selfish memes of our indoctrination . . . We have the power to turn against our creators. We, alone on earth, can rebel against the tyranny of selfish replicators.'

Freudian theory has developed over the eighty years of its existence in so many directions that it is hard to crystallise it into a form that could be disproved. This is one reason for its influence. It was also this characteristic which, in its comparatively early years, led Popper to realise that such a theory which defied refutation, which every observation seemed to confirm, could not be regarded as science. I must repeat that this is not the same as saying it is nonsense. On the contrary it is a fruitful source of ideas; but its predictions tend to be ambiguous and its interpretations cannot be relied upon in the way that reliance was placed on the theories of physics in order to guide man to the moon. Nor does the dismissal of Freudianism as science imply that the psychoanalytic treatment of patients is no good. There is a vital difference between applying Freudian theories in the man-to-man situation of psychoanalytic therapy and applying them to human behaviour at large or to historical characters. In the treatment situation the patient is there to disagree, if he thinks fit, with the analyst's interpretation of his behaviour. In other words the interpretation is subject to criticism, and in that situation the truth may well emerge. In the broader field there is no objective criticism, and conclusions derived from psychoanalytic theory in these circumstances are no more than speculations. The trouble is that, as I shall indicate below, we do rely in the broader field on psychoanalytic speculations, even if not explicitly.

In a paper to the British Association in 1976 Dr William Belson blamed television violence for violent behaviour in real life. The same allegation is now being contested in a case in the American courts. Much emphasis is placed on the fact that Dr Belson and those who agree with him have not been able to prove their thesis. Of course they have not. As we have seen, it is theoretically impossible for them to do so. And not only does this seem to be a failing on their part, it seems to be generally regarded as being up to them to try to do so, rather than for the defenders of television violence to defend their case that it does no harm. Why should it be generally accepted that it does no harm? After all it is a matter of experience that examples are followed. Children imitate their parents and peers, and, even more relevant, sensibilities are blunted by familiarity. Most people feel queasy and many actually faint when present for the first time at a surgical operation on a live human being. But everybody whose job it is to be present gets accustomed to it. Most people are upset when for the first time they see a dead body, but those whose work involves them frequently with dead bodies take them as a matter of course. Hitler's butchers were recruited from the slaughterers of animals, and many of those who had become used to bashing in the skulls of incurable lunatics soon became able to do the same for healthy Jews and political prisoners. So why should it need to be proved that the repeated sight on television of people being brutally assaulted makes one more able to tolerate brutal assault in real life? I think the blame can fairly be put on psychoanalytic theory which has got the better over other theories, probably because of its romantic appeal and the lack of a firm contrary theory.

The psychoanalytic view in this matter is (or was) broadly that we all have a certain amount of innate aggression, just as we all have a certain amount of available physical energy, and this aggression will out. Some believe in the possibility of 'sublimating' into creative channels this aggression, which tends to be thought of rather like steam under pressure, so that it will, as it were, drive an engine rather than merely burst the boilers. Others think that the aggression can be got rid of vicariously; and this is the theory, unlikely as it appears on the face of it, which has caught on. Watching violence on television gets rid of the violence which would otherwise come out in direct action. (This may be unfair to psychoanalysts who may protest that they no longer believe this. But Roberts's view is, I think, right. What matters is what people believe psychoanalysts believe. And, of course, it is even more

absurd if we are in a sense governed by a theory that
nobody any longer believes.) Throughout the ages
humanitarians have considered that violent spectacles –
gladiator fights, bull fights, public executions, cock fights –
especially when presented as entertainment have had a
brutalising effect on the public rather than the opposite;
and this is why at various times they have all been made
illegal in this country. Is there any reason for thinking that
repeated television portrayals of these things might have
the opposite effect? At the bottom of our acceptance of this
illogical position is the attractiveness of romantic,
non-scientific theories such as the Freudian steam-pressure
theory of the mind compared with a hard rational
scepticism, and the failure of our thinkers to face the
public, and especially the students, with this scepticism.
Very largely on the strength of an irrefutable theory, we
are allowing the future generation to grow up in an
atmosphere of sustained portrayed violence after reformers
had, for the previous three hundred years, succeeded in
slowly reducing the amount of public violence permitted.

Because Freudian ideas go very largely against common
sense, their influence has tended to give a kind of boost to
other ideas which, in the ordinary course of events would
have been destroyed by common sense. The influence has
thus been extraordinarily pervasive and difficult to pin
down. Among such ideas which have persisted and can in
some way be attributed to the 'diffused effect' of Freud are
what might be called the infantilising of teaching and the
medicalising of morality.

Teaching methods, developed quite properly on
psychoanalytic lines to overcome the resistance to learning
of backward children of various sorts, have been extended
in many schools to the children who are perfectly willing
to learn, in the spirit of 'a dose of medicine will do them
all good'. In effect all children are being treated as
backward. That play is the best way for children to learn is
another widely assumed idea that owes its popularity to
the Freudians. Peter Smith (1978) casts doubt on it. The
same goes for the 'disproportionate and irreversible' effect
of the early environment on the developing child, criticised
by the Clarkes (1976).

Freudian ideas have combined in a curious way with a bogus egalitarianism to produce the current dogma that competition of any sort in academic performance (but not in sport or music or art) is to be condemned. An aspect of this is the cloud under which 'streaming' in secondary schools is regarded in some quarters. It has resulted in (a) the same thing being done under another name, e.g. 'banding' and (b) in a great outburst of extra-curricular academic competition, especially on radio and television: University Challenge, Ask the Family, etc. A similar tendency to evade such a doctrinaire reversal of tradition is demonstrated by studies of persistent truants from school. They have been found sometimes to organise themselves into gangs where the discipline and punishments are far harsher than in any school.

There has been an attempt to make every misfortune, disability, crime, or eccentricity into a kind of illness subject to diagnosis, treatment, and cure. I am not saying that Freud started the idea, merely that his 'diffused effects' gave it a great fillip. Its absurdity is best illustrated by an extreme example, the psychiatric 'illness' given the name drapetomania by Samuel A. Cartwright MD who first described it, in all seriousness, in the May 1851 issue of the *New Orleans Medical and Surgical Journal*. The symptoms occurred in slaves and manifested themselves as an unexplained tendency to run away. Before the full development of the symptoms, the patient was likely to become sulky and dissatisfied. Treatment by whipping was sometimes effective; but the condition could best be prevented by keeping the patient firmly in the state willed by the Creator, namely that of a 'submissive knee-bender'. The condition was practically confined to the negro race.

Freud cited Hamlet as a kind of archetype of the neurotic; but undoubtedly many so-called neurotics are better typified by Lady Macbeth, and this example shows the dangers of the 'medical model'. Lady Macbeth's obsessional hand-washing was the consequence of her own guilt, not just what Freudians tend to dismiss as guilt-feelings, but real guilt about her dominant part in cold-blooded murder. Her doctor's own comment was entirely apt: 'More needs she the divine than the physician'

(Act V. Sc.1). A successful relief of her guilt might enable her to murder again without feeling guilty, in other words convert her from a woman of sensibility into a psychopath. This is why the pharmaceutical firms' dream of the perfect tranquillizer is not something that doctors await with unequivocal enthusiasm. It could appear to signify the ultimate reduction of morals to chemistry.

The confusion of guilt (for which one can at best make some atonement) with 'guilt-feelings' (which one can be cured of) is part of the blurring of distinctions that I have mentioned which leads to an undermining of truth. Apropos of Rolf Hochhuth's play which seemed to accuse Churchill of having contrived General Sikorski's fatal air crash, a Freudian was heard to say that he was inclined to believe the charge because Churchill was the sort of person who *could* have done it. In one sentence he dismissed centuries of history, of the laborious working up to fair trial in the light of evidence, of being not guilty unless proved guilty. What did it matter, Churchill being the sort of man who might have done it, whether he actually did it or not?

The concept of intelligence

I cannot leave discussion of the anti-cultural influence of modern psychology without mentioning a matter which has nothing to do with Freud and little with Pavlov, the concept of the intelligence quotient, the I.Q. The idea that human mental capacity could be measured by a single number can probably be attributed to Francis Galton, a Victorian pioneer psychologist of immense ability who according to George Miller, 'was never satisfied with a problem until he had discovered something he could count'. To Galton it was so obvious as to be not worth questioning that intellectual capacity is related to the physical dimensions of the brain. Nowadays the idea smacks of Bertie Wooster and makes us smile. (Wodehouse enthusiasts will remember how Bertie was convinced that the explanation for Jeeves's omniscience and amazing competence lay in the way his head bulged out at the back.) It is not a silly idea. It just happens to be wrong, except in the case of brains markedly smaller than average (microcephalic) which always do denote mental defect. Although Galton's attempts to correlate intelligence with brain size were unsuccessful, they led, Miller shows, via Alfred Binet to the I.Q. of today based on standardised tests. 'It seems likely', says Popper, 'that there are innate differences of intelligence. But it seems almost impossible that a matter so many-sided and complex as human inborn knowledge and intelligence (quickness of grasp, depth of understanding, creativity, clarity of exposition, etc.) can be measured by a one-dimensional function like "Intelligence Quotient"' (SB 123). Again, as with brain size, a very low I.Q. does denote mental defect; but Medawar, for one, has suggested that the amount by which the score exceeds a certain amount may be as insignificant as small variations in brain size. We do not know, for example that Einstein or Bertrand Russell had very high I.Q.s. In agreement with this idea, Popper has commented that probably the most difficult intellectual task that any of us ever faces is the learning of his native language. Yet we all achieve it.

The alleged connection between I.Q. and race is a subject on which people have literally come to blows. But the critics of the comparative racial results seem to criticise more the application than the actual concept of the I.Q. which Professor D. H. Stott has described as 'biologically preposterous'. Furious discussions go on under the misapprehension that what are argued about are matters of fact and of science, rather than of metaphysics (see page 20). The I.Q. is, I think one can safely say, a wrong idea which has had the power, as Stott quotes to 'dig the educational graves of many racially and/or economically deprived children for too long'. It has been kept alive by the failure to recognize white-swanning as invalid. Although it is not strictly analogous, the following example does illustrate the white-swanning fallacy. Asked about a friend's new car, the average wife will describe it in terms of colour and perhaps size. To the automobile connoisseur, what are interesting and important are the power and design of the engine, the system of suspension, and other technical details. Nevertheless it can be 'proved' that colour is relevant to performance. The theory that white cars are faster than black can be verified. The tests that have been used to show that black people have on average a lower I.Q. than whites would also show that black cars are on average slower than white ones. Among the explanatory facts of course, which do not emerge from a statistical comparison, are that the police who need fast cars tend to favour white, while undertakers who need slow ones invariably opt for black. Another observation on the same lines is the finding that short-sighted people get higher-paid jobs!

As with I.Q., so with some of the other labels that are pinned on children by psychiatrists and psychologists. They treat poor performances as though they were hereditary diseases. In effect a child who loses at chess lacks the chess-playing ability. Nobody bothers to inquire whether he understands the rules (see also page 132).

In conclusion I must make this point quite clear. To categorise Freudianism or any other theory as metaphysics rather than science is not to deny the truth or even the relevance of observations made by psychoanalysts or anybody else. What must be denied is their power to deduce a general theory of 'human nature' and thereby to make predictions on the score of their observations. For no theory can be deduced from any set of facts. Popper has shown, most ingeniously and by purely logical means, that even so well-tested a theory as Newton's laws of motion could not have been deduced from observation (C.R. 190). Observations can of course suggest an hypothesis; but they cannot prove or confirm a theory. Conclusions from Freudian theory are thus strictly limited in their scope and so, as I shall show in the next chapter, are those from stimulus-response psychology. These theories do not of themselves undermine 'the very foundation of liberal civilisation', and 'the ideal of the rational, responsible, consciously-motivated individual' remains a noble one.

6

Conditioning is an illusion

The second influential group of theories mentioned in the last chapter comprises the stimulus–response psychologies. Pavlov's classical *conditioning* experiment is well known: how by repeatedly sounding a bell before presenting food he induced a dog to salivate to the bell alone. The sound of the bell, an arbitrary neutral *stimulus*, became *conditioned*, producing automatically the same *response* as was reflexly produced by the *unconditioned* stimulus, the smell and sight of food. (This is the 'official' terminology. In popular parlance, of course, it is the animal rather than the stimulus that becomes conditioned.) According to the theory, a new connection was established in the cerebral cortex of the animal by the repetition and association of the experimental procedure.

Running through the subsequent development of the theory is a trend which originated with Thorndike, an American contemporary of Pavlov, and has greatly influenced B. F. Skinner who regards Pavlovian conditioning as of much less importance in human learning than what he now calls *operant* (formerly operant *conditioning*). In contrast with the stimulus substitution of Pavlov, whereby a new conditioned stimulus produces the same response as the unconditioned stimulus, Thorndike's system amounted to a response substitution. A new (usually desired) response is made to the same stimulus: the 'right' speech, note, typewriter key, is substituted for the 'wrong' response previously made to the 'cue'. It is essentially a system of trial and error, success and failure, reward and punishment. This is the basis, it is fair to say, of Skinner's operant – his technical terms – *positive* and *negative reinforcers*, being the equivalent of reward and punishment in the vernacular.

As long ago as 1959, Noam Chomsky published a very long review of Skinner's book *Verbal Behavior* and showed that there was a kind of sleight of hand in Skinner's extrapolation of his carefully controlled experiments with rats in captivity to uncontrolled, everyday, human situations. His most telling point was that, out of the mass of external and internal stimulation to which the individual was subjected and the totality of his behaviour, Skinner picked out single elements and called them *the* stimulus and *the* response and assumed them to be connected, only because this connection fitted both the laboratory results and the theory. Devastating as this criticism was, Skinner went on his way as though nothing had ever been said, indeed he recently revealed to David Cohen that he did not read Chomsky's paper until ten years later.

Popper's refutation of conditioning centres on the idea of repetition. It follows from his rejection of Hume's psychological theory (page 14) that we – humans and animals in general – observe repetitions and then act in the expectation that these repetitions will go on recurring. But, says Popper: 'All repetitions that we experience are approximate repetitions . . . Repetition B of an event A is not identical with A or indistinguishable from A, but only more or less similar to A' (L.Sc.D. 520). Things which are similar but not identical are similar only in certain respects; and whether or not we regard things as being similar depends on whether we are interested in those respects. Popper illustrates his argument with diagrams which show that things may be similar in different respects and that similarity in one respect may easily be accompanied by dissimilarity in another.

A good example is the spuriously objective pick-the-odd-one-out kind of question in which examinees are systematically put in the wrong. Seeing the similarity between the non-odd items presumes a point of view. The question is really 'guess what I am thinking of' and is a good illustration of the need for criticism of experts in general. It is quite inconceivable that the examiner will have considered all the possibilities of similarity and dissimilarity in the words listed; and it is easily conceivable that the examinee

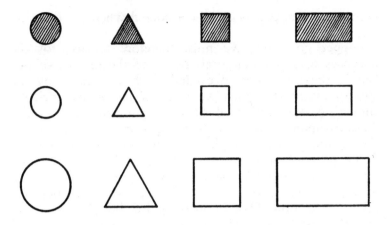

If we look at this diagram, we find that some of the figures are similar with respect to shading (hatching) or to its absence; others are similar with respect to shape; and others are similar with respect to size. The table might be extended like this.

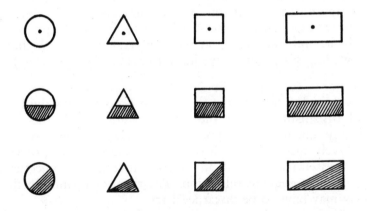

One can easily see that there is no end to the possible kinds of similarity.

Popper's diagrams to illustrate his argument on repetition and similarity

Source: *The Logic of Scientific Discovery*, Karl R. Popper, Hutchinson, Revised Edition 1968, Appendix *x, page 421.

will hit on one that was not considered when the question was set.

Popper goes on: 'We must therefore replace, for the purposes of a psychological theory of the origins of our beliefs, the naive idea of events which *are* similar by the idea of events to which we react by *interpreting* them as similar' (C.R.45). For all of us seeing things as similar depends upon interpretation, anticipation, and expectation. We cannot therefore explain anticipation and expectation as being consequences of repetition. For even the first repetition-for-us would only be interpreted as such if it is seen as similar, and seeing something as similar depends upon expectation. Thus Popper was led, he said, by purely logical considerations to replace Hume's widely assumed, weaker, psychological theory of induction with the following:

> Without waiting passively for repetitions to impress or impose regularities on us, we actively try to impose regularities on the world. We try to discover similarities in it, and interpret it in terms invented by us. Without waiting for premises we jump to conclusions. (C.R.46)

Pavlov's dog invents the theory that food follows the bell. All organisms are all the time inventing such theories, mainly unconsciously but actively. The theories are not passively instilled into them by the 'conditioning' process. It is essentially a trial and error process, of conjectures open to subsequent refutation. The theories formed in this way may have to be discarded later.

Skinner's operant behaviour can, as I have mentioned, also be regarded as a trial and error process and may therefore seem to come to the same thing as what Popper describes. The vital difference is that Skinner does not allow that the spontaneous action, the trial, can be theory-directed, intelligently exploratory. He rules out of court the intervention of thoughts, ideas, theories, intentions. He does not deny that they exist; but regards them as mere 'flotsam' accompanying the action. For him the trial in trial-and-error is not based on conjecture. It is blind and random; and words are nothing but the movement of the vocal cords.

This is another of those conceptual illusions that I mentioned in the first chapter (page 17): conspiracy, induction, instruction, and now, it looks as though the world imposes its pattern on the passive organism, but really the active organism tries out its guesses on the world and the world accepts or rejects them. In the physical world perhaps the best example of the same sort of thing is suction. There is no such thing as suction, conceived as a magnet-like force. When you 'suck' up lemonade through a straw what really happens of course is that the atmospheric pressure forces some of the liquid up the straw into the region of lowered, but positive, pressure in your mouth. What looks like pull is really push. However the idea of suction remains convenient fiction as long as it is not taken too far – more than about thirty-four feet for water. The most powerful pump imaginable will not 'suck' water from a greater depth than that. It is important to mention this fact that a false theory can be useful within some range, but manifestly and dangerously false outside that range. I can best illustrate this by adapting an example used by Popper in a slightly different context. Suppose the time is really five minutes past eleven. Then the statement 'It is eleven o'clock' is untrue but more useful for *most* purposes than the true statement 'It is between ten o'clock and midday'. However the generally useful eleven o'clock statement is a dangerous one for the purpose of catching a train timed to depart at 11.04. Newtonian physics, which is grossly inaccurate when velocities of the same order as that of light are concerned, is more useful than Einsteinian physics in the ordinary 'practical' range.

But to return to the case in point, Popper's rejection of conditioning is of a piece with a central element in his philosophy, that there is no such thing as direct experience. The central mistake, he says, in the so-called commonsense theory of knowledge is the quest for certainty, which leads to 'the singling out . . . of sense data or sense impressions or immediate experiences as a secure basis of all knowledge. But . . . these data or elements do not exist at all. They are the inventions', he adds, 'of hopeful philosophers, who have managed to bequeath them to the psychologists' (O.K.63).

He reaches his conclusion by logical means but the view that what seems to be directly experienced is really the result of interpretation of coded information is of course a fact of anatomy and physiology. At birth our brains are in the position of an underground military intelligence unit connected with the outside world only by telephone lines, most of which are unlabelled. Only by a lengthy process of cross reference can the brain attach labels so it can tell, at once and reliably, whence any particular message originates. Recent research on the eye has underlined the degree to which the brain interprets rather than merely receives data. The eye is, in optical terms, a very poor sort of camera, producing an extremely fuzzy image, much less clear than what we 'see'. The brain compares the series of blurred images as the eye scans and deduces the clear image we 'see' and even after years of experience we can still be deceived by 'optical illusions'.

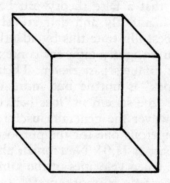

The Necker cube, illustrated here, demonstrates two facts that are central to the theme of this book. The first is the one mentioned above that there is no such thing as direct experience. There are no sensory data corresponding to the bits of information that are stored in a computer. All perceptions are interpretations of coded signals, analogous to the reading of a non-standardized Morse code. The second fact is that the will or conscious intention can sometimes override unconscious reaction. The figure is clearly a network of straight lines in a plane, but we perceive it as a three-dimensional figure in space. If one fixes one's gaze so that the lower square appears to be the front face of the cube, then after less than thirty seconds one's perception involuntarily changes so that the upper square becomes the front face. However one can intentionally override this and switch back to the original perception – and back again if so desired.

The above by no means exhaust the reasons against what Popper calls the bucket theory of the mind, the idea that experience is just passively collected. Above all there is the mechanism of attention whereby of the mass of sensory material reaching the brain at any one time, only a fraction is admitted to consciousness. What is perceived depends upon attention, upon interest, and upon what has previously been perceived. To a degree we see what we are watching and hear what we are listening to. This is yet another of the same kind of illusion: it looks like direct experience, but it is really interpretation.

'There is no such thing as association or conditioned reflex', wrote Popper (O.K.67), and he later amplified the statement: 'I do not at all question the correctness of the "conditioning" and "reinforcement", and "learning" *experiments*; but I give them and the learning process a different interpretation' (personal communication). The wealth of observation that has accumulated from learning experiments is not invalidated by the suspicion that conditioning and association are untenable hypotheses, but the observations will need reinterpretation in the light of a better theory. And I cannot help suspecting that some experimental results which have been presented as though they were universal phenomena will turn out to be singular events.

Eysenck made a revealing admission in his account of J. B. Watson's 'little Albert' experiment, commonly regarded as a classic in the application of conditioning theory to the treatment of the neuroses. By hitting an iron bar with a hammer whenever Albert reached out to touch a white rat, Watson gave him a pathological fear of white rats and other small furry animals. However, Eysenck says: 'Watson was lucky in his choice of subject; others have

banged away with hammers on metal bars in an attempt to
condition infants, but not always with the same success.'
Other accounts of this experiment have been less frank
than Eysenck's (e.g. Salter and Wolpe), and have allowed it
to be assumed that conditioning of this sort is as
predictable as a chemical reaction. Eysenck explains the
failure in terms of the great variation of inherited
'conditionability'. A simpler, Popperian, explanation might
be that what was repetition-for-Albert was not
repetition-for-everybody.

Interestingly enough, Skinner in his interview with
David Cohen makes the same kind of admission with
regard to Pavlov. 'He was dealing with . . . just about the
only gland that would have worked. It's an amazing
accident that he hit on it. It's very hard to find another
gland that could be used . . . You can't use tears. You
probably could have used some other gastric secretions if
you could get at them more easily. But I doubt that you
could use urine or sweat. Salivation was it. As a matter of
fact . . . you might say that Pavlov was a specialist in
conditioned salivation.'

The conditioning *experiments* are not questioned, nor is it
denied here that the theory can be useful in practice, just as
rules of thumb are useful – often more useful than exact
calculations. What must be dismissed is the tendency to say
'this is all there is to human behaviour – stimulus and
response, positive and negative reinforcement'. It is the
fanciful and naive generalisations of a philosophical nature,
allegedly deduced from conditioning theory (itself perhaps
a generalisation from the salivation of dogs), that must be
firmly rejected; generalisations which pose as 'proof' that
traditional values and ideas of truth and free will can no
longer be taken seriously by those who consider themselves well informed and up to date. I am thinking of such
works as B. F. Skinner's *Beyond Freedom and Dignity*,
Nigel Calder's book and television series *The Mind of Man*,
and an article in *New Scientist* entitled 'The shadow of the
mind' by Professor John Taylor.

'Physiological' psychology, a new discipline started
independently by Pavlov in Russia and Thorndike in the

U.S.A. at the end of the nineteenth century, was a reaction against the earlier introspective psychology which was criticised as subjective and therefore unscientific. The raison d'être of the new science was its objectivity. Its extreme proponents took the view that only what could be independently observed existed. It is ironical that they should have enthroned as their central concept this conditioning process, this unobservable and perhaps mythical process in the cerebral cortex.

What I hope I have demonstrated in these two chapters is that the current tendency to explain all human thought and behaviour in terms of (unsubstantiated) theories of unconscious psychology tends, in the first place, to distract from the central importance of rationality and reasonableness and conscious responsibility, which as I have already shown form the only known alternative to violence, as well as being our peculiarly human qualities. In the second place the cult of psychology distracts from the practical things that can be done to improve our society by way of improving its institutions and inventing new ones. We cannot change human psychology but we can change our institutions, little by little, and – to use the phrase already quoted – these can make an incalculable difference to human happiness.

7

The straitjacket of planning

On the 28th of July 1914 all the great European powers were at peace. By the 4th of August all but Italy were at war. According to A. J. P. Taylor's account of that week, in itself hilarious if one forgets the fearful consequences, the politicians 'were dragged into war by their armies, instead of using the armies to further their policies'. The armies in their turn were dragged by their plans and by the railway timetables.

To take just the example of Germany: their war plans had been devised by Count von Schlieffen to cope with one problem only, the war on two fronts. Since his death in 1908 they had hardly been looked at, let alone revised. They were: first to attack France and encircle the French armies on the German frontier by a right hook through Belgium; then, having defeated France, to turn their attention to Russia. There was no provison for doing it the other way round. 840,000 men were to be sent by train into Belgium, all though the one railway junction of Aachen; but they could not stop there. The trains had to go on to clear the lines for more trains to come. There was no possibility of stopping at the frontier.

The Kaiser and his Foreign Minister, Bethmen Hollweg, imagined that they could rattle their swords without actually drawing them, as rulers had so often done before. They had no idea how their freedom of action had been constrained by Schlieffen's plan. 'They never asked, and the generals never told them.' After the Kaiser had declared war on Russia on August 1st, he was told that Sir Edward Grey had said that Great Britain would remain neutral if Germany would not attack France. Wilhelm was delighted and called for champagne. But Schlieffen's successor, von Moltke, 'turned pale and said "It is impossible" '. On learning of Russia's mobilisation, he had, Taylor says, 'opened the drawer of his desk and followed Schlieffen's instructions'. 1,100 trains were now on their way, as ordained by the timetable drawn up years before. They could not be halted without throwing the army into confusion. So the Kaiser signed the mobilisation orders against France and justified them by ordering his own planes to raid Nuremberg, pretending that they were French.

The story was similar, although less absurd, in all the other countries. The essence of it was this: the Russians could not make a gesture in support of Serbia against Austria–Hungary, because partial mobilisation against Austria–Hungary (which was all that Suzanov, the Foreign Minister, wanted) would have delayed for months (because of *their* railway timetables) their capability of mobilising against Germany, should this prove necessary later. So Russia ordered full mobilisation. Germany, as we have seen, could not respond to this threat (which was not meant to be a threat to her), without first attacking and defeating both Belgium and France; and Britain could not go to the aid of Belgium (which was all that she wanted to do) without allying herself with France.

Unknown to Russia and Serbia, the Austro–Hungarian threat against Serbia which provoked the Russian mobilisation could not be carried out for various reasons, one of which was that they dared not commit their army in that direction without being sure of Russian neutrality; and 'as a little extra twist of irony' Serbia's decision (unknown of course to both Austria–Hungary and Russia) was not to resist, should Austria–Hungary march on Belgrade.

All these moves and constrictions were imposed by the military plans and had nothing much to do with the personalities or wills of the politicians and generals in office at the time. Indeed in each country the plans prevented the statesmen from doing what they wanted to do. World 3 controlled World 2 and World 1.

It is often said that if only all politicians could be psychoanalysed and freed from their complexes and 'hang-ups', there would be no more war. But on this story, even allowing for some oversimplification, it seems that Freud himself, had he changed places (at this stage) with the Kaiser or Grey, would have found it hard to act otherwise than they did. They were held in the straitjacket of their own plans and were powerless to wriggle free. It was the plans that sent ten million soldiers and ultimately twice as many civilians to their deaths.

I retell this story because it clearly still has lessons for us. One might have thought that everybody would have second thoughts for ever more about making long term plans to restrict freedom of action in the future. But in this country at any rate, thousands of people are beavering away as hard as they can doing just that, producing straitjackets for the future, the worst (that we know about!) being the structure plans, which, under the Town and Country Planning Act of 1971, local authorities were to combine together to produce, for roughly county-sized areas.

In the case of South Hampshire, the structure plan had to be radically altered even before it was submitted to the Department of the Environment because the population predictions made only a few years before were already obviously false. One of the worst features of the new arrangement was that the new plans were to take on board as 'commitments' the current plans of the previously-existing, smaller, planning authorities. In the case of South Hampshire, some two hundred such commitments were incorporated into the structure plan without further consideration. A Portsmouth scheme, rapidly becoming notorious, known as stage III of the North–South Road (N/S III), was one of these so-called commitments. Had these old plans remained under the auspices of the authorities who thought them up in the first place, many would have been cancelled or modified or would have died a natural death. Now, not only were the plans themselves given a new lease of life and enhanced status as part of a new and altogether grander plan, but the same kiss of life was extended to the planning *ideas*, many of them by now discredited, on which the plans had been based. For example N/S III had been based on theories of traffic growth and life of houses current in the early 1960s and no longer accepted (see page 110). Furthermore it had been planned before bus priority measures had been thought of, before there was any general concern about an impending energy crisis, and before the 1972–4 quadrupling of world oil prices. Yet although the population growth assumptions on which N/S III was based were even more outdated than those of the structure plan itself, the former was perpetuated and the latter modified. The perpetuation of these old plans has made it almost impossible, without endless bureaucratic unscrambling, to do what seems to be sensible now. We are hamstrung by the plans just as were the Kaiser and von Moltke.

The same Act that gave us the structure plans ordained also that there would follow local plans for smaller areas conforming to the 'strategic' outline of the structure plan. Ever since 1972 the planners in Portsmouth have been endeavouring to produce a Fratton Centre Local Plan for the area through which N/S III is planned to run. A draft was published in that year and was hastily withdrawn, as it at once met a storm of objection. Its gestation continued behind the scenes for a further six years, during which it cast a continued blight on the area and during which several major decisions – for the road and for other land use – were taken without it. The plan's central features were the pedestrianisation of the main shopping street which is the main traffic route for the area and the redevelopment (to include multi-storey car park and new department store) of the largest central block. Both these features had to be withdrawn (the first because of council members' opposition and the second because of developer's cold feet) as soon as the council were given a preview and before general publication. But the plan goes on, shorn of its raison d'être, and consisting now of a hundred or so parochial decisions about parcels of land mostly of less than an acre: a bit of car parking here, build a few houses there – all decisions to be taken now on matters where decisions could better be taken on an ad hoc basis or when need arises. It is truly a matter of trying hard to prevent posterity from doing as it thinks best.

As an illustration of how current planning encumbered by the ideas of the 1960s can indulge in most of the errors enumerated in this book, I cite in some detail the case of part of the Fratton Plan area of Portsmouth, an area about 300 yards square now known as the Cumberland Road area. In 1965 the council decided, as did many others, on a road plan to meet the anticipated needs of 1985. Before I describe this I must explain, for the benefit of non-mathematicians, the confusion of linear and exponential growth, which has bedevilled so many plans for the future. If 1,000 things increase in one year to 1,100, you may say with equal truth either that there has been an increase of 100 or of 10 per cent. If there is a regular increase each year of 100, we have linear growth and the original 1,000 will double itself in 10 years. But a second annual increase of 10 per cent will be 10 per cent of 1,100, that is 110, and the third year 121 and so on. Exponential growth at 10 per cent will double itself in about $7\frac{1}{2}$ years. Not very much difference so far. But as time goes on there is rapid divergence. While the linear growth will treble the original in 20 years and quadruple in 30, the exponential will treble in about $11\frac{1}{2}$ and quadruple in about $14\frac{1}{2}$.

When something new is introduced, such as cars in a country where there are none, or electricity to a country dependent on candles, the growth at first is likely to be exponential. But as demand begins to be satisfied or restriction on growth begins – most people already have electric lights and a cooker, or traffic congestion starts – that growth tends to become linear and later still tails off to a plateau of no growth.

Portsmouth planners assumed, on the strength of recent annual increases, an exponential growth rate of traffic for the next twenty years of 5 per cent per annum, which would mean rather more than $2\frac{1}{2}$ times as much traffic in 1985 as in the planning year, 1965. In fact the growth in the number of registered vehicles between 1966 and 1976 was almost exactly linear and the growth of traffic rather less than linear. This can be explained by the fact that as car ownership increases, more and more of it is accounted for by people having two or even three cars; and they cannot drive them all at once.

To return now to the Cumberland Road area: it consists of four parallel 'Coronation Street' type streets, bounded on one side by the railway and on the other three by comparatively main streets, bus routes and so on. It is in fact exceptionally well served by public transport as well as being within easy walking distance of all the city's amenities. It is thus an ideal residential area for families without cars. (One of the chief planner's reasons for wanting to knock it all down now was the absence of garages and off-street parking!)

The 1965 road plan envisaged the sweeping away of this entire area of some 400 houses (which were then doomed anyway, as, according to the theory then prevailing, they had 'outlived their useful life'.) In the centre would be a four acre roundabout where would intersect a new north–south highway (N/S III) of four lanes with an east–west highway also of four lanes. At a later stage (but before 1985) a further four lanes of north–south highway built on stilts would 'fly over' the roundabout. In the years after 1965, pieces of the ambitious network were completed and other pieces, including the east–west road, were lopped off and cancelled; but N/S III was neither built nor cancelled. It remained as 'part of the programme' to blight all the houses contained in it. Gradually owners sold out to the council who spent little or nothing on the upkeep of the houses they bought, because they were 'short-life' properties. However, as the avalanche of traffic predicted in the early 1960s (see page 110) failed to materialise, the scale of the plans was reduced from the eight lanes on two levels for the north–south road in 1965 to six lanes on one level in 1973, to four lanes in 1976 and in 1978 to a single carriageway. Meanwhile the state of the houses steadily deteriorated and so did the social atmosphere, as the council boarded up some houses, moved in so-called problem families to occupy others, and themselves rendered still others uninhabitable.

An eight-lane highway is a very inflexible thing. Had a

road on that scale been necessary then the site and route for it were reasonable. But once the scale is reduced to single carriageway, you are dealing with something quite manoeuvrable. From that moment it becomes possible to take the road wherever it will do least damage, and that is usually along the route of existing roads. But the plan for an eight-lane route, made in 1965, was for a road through the Cumberland Road area. So through that area must go the single carriageway planned in 1978 to be built in 1981. Sticking to this route is justified by the state of the houses; and demolition of the houses, rather than renovating them as other similar houses elsewhere are being renovated, is justified by the road plan. The reduction of scale has meant a slight change of route for the road, so that some houses which have been empty for six years waiting for the road will not now be needed for it, while one end of a terrace, occupied and in good condition, will now after all be needed for the road. The other end of this well-maintained terrace will be cut off so they 'might as well' be demolished and the land given to an adjacent school which is short of play space.

So the route for the road is justified by the state of the houses and the demolition of the houses is justified by the road plan. And the expansion of the school in that direction rather than any other is justified by the road. Nothing is done for its own sake; and where there are real problems, they are ignored or made worse. The only housing problem, namely where to find houses for old people who need them, will be exacerbated by the plan, which will not only remove renewable old houses but will gobble up land on which new ones might be built. There is no traffic problem in the Cumberland Road area. Elsewhere there are junctions which urgently need traffic lights; but they cannot have them because all the money is earmarked for the road. Even on the line of the road there is a crossroads which causes hold-ups. A roundabout would clear the trouble and there is enough waste land nearby for this to be done; but it is not done. We must have the whole scheme or nothing. The Schlieffen-like road plan prevents people from doing now what seems sensible.

We have here four of the errors: solutioneering – a plan without a clear statement of a problem; trendism – a plan based on a trend which was miscalculated and did not continue; tunnel-vision – a road plan which looks only at theoretical good effects and ignores the unfavourable consequences such as obstuction of cross traffic; and holism – refusal to make minor but genuine improvements before the whole plan is put into effect, for fear that they might make the whole patently unnecessary.

The north–south road was planned to have been built between 1970 and 1975. Part of the reason for the delay has been the admitted uncertainty of the traffic forecasts. We have been waiting for the result of the South Hampshire Transportation Study, based on a highly technical computerised model, which would finally tell us if such a road was really needed 'for the 1980s and 90s'. We have had to wait a long time, and now that it is here the answer is a lemon.

The study, it now transpires, was based on three alternative assumptions, one – maximum investment in highways, two – maximum investment in public transport, and a third intermediate one whose details need not concern us here. On the face of it, allowing for some scepticism about both the input and the method (in view especially of COBA's errors – see page 125) these seemed sensible assumptions. It is only now, when the results are emerging, that we find that the second alternative was not, as everyone had assumed, investment in ordinary buses and trains. On the contrary, in the model investment these remained constant. The idea was to invest in two lengths of segregated semi-automatic light tramcars of an unspecified and untried type. These two lengths of track, even if 'cost-effective', could not hope to affect more than a small part of the thirty-mile long area of the study, but would swallow up all the money. Why did they not test the model of a maximum bus investment programme which was what many people would have voted for? The answer appears to be that the modelling procedure could not be adapted to this possibility. So we are likely to be saddled with a transport plan 'to take us into the twenty-first century' which excludes a practicable alternative, because it cannot be modelled on the computer.

* * *

Of course there are matters on which we have to take decisions now in regard to preparing for the future and there are, in general, three ways of doing this.

1 We can assume that the future will be like the past or, if not exactly so, that *trends* in the recent past will continue into the future in roughly the same way. This is the way in which evolution prepares for the future. It produces for future use the combination of genes that have been successful in the past.

2 We can use our intelligence to produce the best theory about the future, try to see how the future is likely to differ from the past and its trends, e.g. we can see how certain trends cannot continue because of such things as exhaustion of resources, saturation of demand, etc.

3 We can plan to bring about certain changes that seem desirable, but which will happen only with active human intervention by such things as legislation.

I cannot elaborate on these options here. I shall content myself with citing a case at present in dispute between the government and the Central Electricity Generating Board. It illustrates the dilemma, which does not seem to be recognised as a dilemma because of the prevailing trendism.

It concerns the proposal for a new power station on Inswork Point near Plymouth. The C.E.G.B. want to build an oil-fired station there. The government's alternative seems to be a high-voltage transmission line to meet the projected deficiency in the west country by drawing on the surplus of generating capacity which exists in the country as a whole (see page 149).

If we do either of these things the west country will be provided with an electricity supply to meet the demand estimated *on the current trends*. Once the provision has been made by either means (at considerable cost) then it will be in the interests of the supply industry, and therefore ultimately of electricity consumers everywhere and therefore of the country as a whole, that the demand shall materialise. In other words we shall have lost the opportunity to *reduce* the demand for electricity.

An alternative policy would be to grasp the opportunity to try out in this area one or several means which appear now as desirable to meet the crisis of the future. Either separately or together we could

1 Cut down the total energy demand by an active heat-insulation policy financed by the government. (In the case of a badly insulated house reducing heating requirement by one kilowatt cost about £20, at 1976 prices, while a new nuclear generating station cost about £400 per kilowatt of generating capacity, according to the Energy Research Group of the Open University.)

2 Cut down electricity demand by using (with financial encouragement) other fuels for heating, e.g. North Sea gas now, to be replaced as necessary by gas from coal (for heating purposes, twice as efficient as other means of using coal).

3 Instead of building one large power station, build a number of smaller (Combined Heat and Power, CHP) stations. These would be less efficient as producers of electricity but, regarded as heat stations producing electricity as a by-product, much more efficient in the overall utilization of energy, about 70 per cent as compared with a little over 30 per cent. There are of course well known difficulties in using the heat.

If either Inswork or the transmission line is built then they actively inhibit the longer term, energy-conserving solutions of 1, 2, and 3 above. For once the investment is made, it is wasteful not to use it.

In spite of widespread disillusion with the achievements of the planners, many people *still* believe that what is wrong is the attitude and competence of the planners themselves rather than that their aspirations are unrealistic. I think that Popper's work shows that no improvement in technique can possibly realise what planners all over the country are still trying to achieve. Their goal is theoretically – not just practically – impossible.

Two of Popper's propositions are basic to the appreciation of this impossibility. One has already been quoted:

> While it is easy to centralize power, it is impossible to centralize all the knowledge which is distributed over many minds, and whose centralization would be necessary for the wise wielding of centralized power. (P.H.90)

The second proposition is that the growth of human knowledge is essentially unpredictable.

> Tomorrow, or a year hence, we may propose and test important theories of which nobody has seriously thought so far. If there is growth of knowledge in this sense, then it cannot be predictable by scientific means. For he who could so predict our discoveries of tomorrow could make them today. (O.K.298)

A trivial example might be that anybody making traffic plans for cities today is likely to consider including some bus-only routes. But nobody making plans in 1950 for the city of the seventies would have included such routes, for the simple reason that the idea had not then been suggested.

Even in such comparatively straightforward matters as the need for international airports and the costs of large engineering developments (I am thinking of Stansted and Concorde) – just to mention two areas where the greatest expertise has been mustered on prediction – the forecasts have surprisingly soon been shown to be uselessly inaccurate. It is not incompetence or deceit on the part of the forecasters; it is that matters like these, in which human behaviour and human knowledge play a large part, are inherently unpredictable.

When it comes to the replanning of major cities and whole counties and it is a matter not just of estimating future road and housing needs or provision of leisure facilities, but of combining all these and many other highly unpredictable items (including such imponderables as what people are going to want) – not just for the next ten years, but for the rest of the century – then the forecasts become worse than useless. To follow them may be worse than doing nothing, because the result of the vast expenditure and the uprooting of people from their homes may be even less acceptable to posterity than if nothing at all were done now.

We are beginning to realize that, beyond a certain point, motorways generate more traffic and are self-defeating. The next step is to realise something similar in regard to planning. The moment planning goes beyond the eradication of present evils, such as getting rid of slums or dangerous road junctions, or goes beyond what has successfully been done before; the moment it becomes utopian and starts to plan the ideal city of the future, it ceases to be rational. It starts to make assumptions that are called predictions. It feeds these bogus figures into computers and compounds the original errors. The wider the scope of the plan, the greater the snags that *are* not and *cannot* be foreseen. The surmounting of these requires ad hoc adjustments to the plan, and we are back at Popper's 'notorious phenomenon of *unplanned planning*'. (P.H. 69).

Popper thinks that the hankering of modern planners – and politicians – after sweeping reforms has an aesthetic basis, it is associated 'with the desire to build a world which is not only a little better and more rational than ours, but which is free from its ugliness, not a crazy quilt, an old garment badly patched, but an entirely new gown, a really beautiful new world'. He sympathises with this attitude and thinks that most of us 'suffer a little from such dreams of perfection'; but he regards it as a dangerous enthusiasm. Whether it derives from Plato or not it is akin to his attitude to politics. 'Politics, to Plato', Popper said,

is the Royal Art. It is an art – not in a metaphorical sense in which we speak of . . . the art of getting things done, but in a more literal sense. It is an art of composition, like music, painting, or architecture. The Platonist politician composes cities, for beauty's sake.

But, Popper protests:

> I do not believe that human lives may be the means for satisfying an artist's desire for self-expression . . . Much as I sympathise with the aesthetic impulse, I suggest that the artist might seek expression in another material . . . dreams of beauty have to submit to the necessity of helping men in distress and men who suffer injustice. (O.S.165)

Jane Jacobs, in her justly influential book *The Death and Life of Great American Cities*, echoes this sentiment: 'To approach a city, or even a city neighbourhood', she says, 'as if it were a large architectural problem, capable of being given order by converting it into a disciplined work of art, is to make the mistake of substituting art for life.'

In the next chapter I look at some of the results of the surrender to the passion for sweeping physical reforms, although the aesthetic element in them is rather hard to discern.

8

The concrete Jerusalem

Science and democracy are both essentially anti-authoritarian, both depend on freely available infor-mation and freedom of discussion and criticism. We have already seen how the process of planning has mushroomed beyond all sense. In this chapter I shall show how the plans have too often been based on untested, bogus theories, sometimes beyond the criticism of the public because based on computerised analysis of statistics; and the execution of the plans has been undemocratic in the extreme. Things would have been very different had it been publicly and officially recognised that holism and prediction of the future state of society are impossible dreams; and that theories cannot be accepted until they have stood up to public attempts to falsify them.

We are emerging from a decade in which cities all over the country have been literally torn apart in the name of three novel causes; comprehensive redevelopment, highrise flats, and urban motorways. These ideas were foisted on the public by the professions concerned, with the connivance of all the political parties and entirely without any popular democratic demand. If in some matters there is doubt about what the people want, this was not one of them. What people wanted and still want is a house with a bit of garden or at least a back yard. It was implied, although not often explicitly stated, and certainly never proved, that this was impossible unless they were content to be farmed out from their cities to bleak outlying housing estates. The way slum clearance and the redevelopment of central areas of the older cities was carried out in defiance of the wishes of the people was as arrogant as in any dictatorship. The result has been the provision on a vast scale of housing of a type that practically nobody wants. In Portsmouth, which has about 27,000 council dwellings, the housing department themselves acknowledge that there are 8,000 families with young children living in flats and maisonettes, nearly all built since the second world war, which are not suitable for them. Meanwhile the Council are trying to go ahead with a road scheme (page 200) which will destroy some 400 houses with gardens, all built before the first world war, and precisely what the families want.

Shaw once said that every profession was a conspiracy against the public; but of none has this been more true than of the unholy alliance of planners, housing officers, and architectural departments of local authorities, aided and abetted by the then Ministry of Housing and Local Government.

As long ago as 1932 this was written (by Hitchcock and Johnson) of 'international style' housing:

> It implies preparation not for a given family but for a typical family. This statistical monster, the typical family, has no personal existence and cannot defend itself against the sociological theories of the architects . . . The idealism of the functionalists too often demands that they provide what ought to be needed, even at the expense of what is actually needed. Instead of facing the difficulties of the present, they rush on to face the uncertain future.

– a typical combination of holism and historicism.

On the other hand, as recently as 1941 George Orwell described us as

> a nation of stamp collectors, pigeon fanciers, amateur carpenters, coupon snippers, darts players, crossword-puzzle fans. All the culture which is most truly native centres round things which even when they are communal are not official – the pub, the football match, the backgarden, the fireside.

Now, through no choice of their own, for very many there

is no back garden, no place in which to pursue these characteristic hobbies – and no fireside either.

As though all this was not enough, there was an added element of uglification in much that was done. Not only were many of the new buildings constructed of some sort of preformed concrete panels, but there was a deliberate disregard by architects and planners of aesthetic detail, proportion, and above all, scale. Jeremy Bugler described in the *Observer* how one particular building featured 'a massive lift and ventilator shaft, looking like nothing so much as a lift and ventilator shaft'. And this was typical. The idea that one facet of art is deception, the calculated creation of illusion, was scorned in favour of what was called 'honesty' in design. A high rise office block would be placed next to a listed regency house and visually destroy it, just as the stock exchange and its companion monstrosities have destroyed the grandeur of St Paul's.

Nor, in spite of their honesty, were the buildings any better in respect of their primary function of keeping out the weather. What the layman calls leaks and the expert 'water penetration' occurred all too frequently, partly because of a fashion for flat roofs instead of the traditional pitched variety which is not only virtually foolproof for keeping out the rain but also effective in keeping the heat in in winter and out in summer. They were plagued too, owing to a general ignorance of physics, by condensation, leading to great growths of mould; but this was usually blamed on the occupants in that they did too much washing, bathing, and breathing. At least half of the 523 houses, maisonettes, and flats in Portsdown Park, a Portsmouth municipal housing scheme designed in 1965, have let in the rain (and hundreds are still doing so), some so badly as to make it dangerous to switch on the ceiling lights in wet weather. The architects were the winners of a nationally organised competition, and their scheme later won a design award! Four blocks, each of 136 flats, in another scheme just fifteen years old, built by the Bison system, are now shedding lumps of concrete and having to be repaired at a total cost of at least £2½ million. According to *Building Design* (20 October 1978) nearly 50,000 flats of this type were built throughout the country. The London Borough of Hillingdon which has 1,450 of them is in perhaps the greatest trouble.

A public, who during the war had reacted with indignation at what were called the Baedeker raids – air attacks on selected cathedral cities, looked on dumbly as the bulldozers cut swathes right up to the cathedral closes in Canterbury, Worcester, and Salisbury. And the almost unrelieved dreariness of the new buildings together with the legalized vandalism of the demolition squads invited and were answered by illegal vandalism on a scale never seen before. In two lines Sir John Betjeman said it all:

Goodbye to old Bath! We who loved you are sorry.
They've carted you off by developer's lorry.

At the heart of the matter were two theories, assumed but hardly criticised, two bogeys which, at the beginning of the 1960s, frightened both central government and local authorities into ill-considered and precipitate action. One was the theory that all the houses built before 1900 would have to be replaced in the near future, and the other was the prediction of a tidal wave of motor traffic. The spectre of cities being swamped by a deluge of cars was given a special fillip by the publication in 1963 of the Buchanan Report *Traffic in Towns*, an absurd futuristic fantasy. It is hard now to believe that it was ever taken seriously. (Later, in 1972, Buchanan wrote: 'I have yet to see anything that has taken my breath away as it was taken away when I first saw the German autobahnen in 1937'.) His 1963 report was seized on by municipal planners and engineers all over the country and used to scare their councils into letting them lay waste their cities more thoroughly than the German bombers had done twenty years before. In Portsmouth, for example, the development officer reported to the city council in 1964 as follows: 'The report [Buchanan] reveals the startling fact [sic] that the number of cars may be expected to double by 1970 and treble by 1980.' It was not a fact. Total vehicle registrations in 1963 were 12 million, and they rose only to 14.93 million in 1970.

It was not even a fact that that was what Buchanan had predicted, though he too was wildly out in only seven years. He had predicted 18 million by 1970 – *nearly* double the *1960* figure of 9½ million. 18 million was not reached until 1976.

There was no question in the reports of the early 1960s of not trying to accommodate the expected flood of traffic. There was an implicit view of traffic as comparable to sewage, something whose flow one simply dared not attempt to constrict. There was also the fear of the total seize up, with all traffic grinding to a halt. Nobody ever seemed to ask the question: what will happen if we do not build all these roads? The only traffic experts had trained as road builders. The only way they knew for coping with traffic was to build new roads or widen the old ones.

It was not until Jane Jacob's great iconoclastic, anti–planning classic reached this country that people came to their senses and realised that traffic is an assemblage of vehicles, each dependent on an individual driver's decision as to whether to go this way or that or to leave his car at home. She described a case in New York where the protesters against the plan for a new highway which would bisect their residential area succeeded not only in stopping it but also in closing to through traffic the existing main route. Contrary to the experts' predictions that the consequence would be a surge of traffic down residential side roads, there was in fact a reduction of traffic there too.

Jane Jacobs also brought a breath of economic reality into the planners' dream of having everything new. 'If a city area has only new buildings, the enterprises that can exist there are automatically limited to those that can support the high costs of construction . . . only operations that are well–established, high–turnover, standardized or heavily subsidized . . . chain stores, chain restaurants, and banks . . .' Planners have failed to realize that in tearing down every old building they have stifled the emergence of new enterprises. 'As for really new ideas of any kind – no matter how profitable or successful some of them might ultimately be – there is no leeway for chancy trial, error, and experimentation, in the high–overhead economy

of new construction.' She sums it up with the aphorism:
'Old ideas can sometimes use new buildings. New ideas
must use old buildings.'

The two bogeys – short life of houses and traffic
avalanche – worked together to further the cause of the
urban motorway mania. Councillors who might have
jibbed at the idea of destroying hundreds of perfectly good
homes for roads, felt differently when told that the houses
have to come down in a few years anyway, so why not
now? Phrases such as 'nearing the end of their useful life'
and 'ripe for redevelopment' were used to imply that it
was kinder to destroy these houses now, like lame horses,
than allow them to crumble of old age in a few years'
time. Now, in contrast with the idea of the 1960s that
hundred-year-old houses would have to come down, some
local authorities, while energetically rehabilitating their
nineteenth century houses, are having to contemplate
demolition of their highrise tenements only twenty years old.

If anybody doubts that what we have just witnessed was
a fashion and not rational action, he has only to consider
one of the arguments for highrise which was swallowed by
councils all over the country. It was that you could not get
the required density of population per acre with low- or
medium-rise development. Although the facts on which
the calculation was based have not changed, architects now
generally accept that this is not true; and this changed
opinion is born out by the fact that the density is roughly
the same in the Somers Town area of Portsmouth, rebuilt
between 1964 and '66 largely with 18-storey blocks of flats,
as it is in phase 2 of the Buckland area of the same city,
rebuilt in the early 1970s with one 7-storey block and
many two-storey houses. More absurd was the programme
of new roads for Greater Manchester. 75 per cent of it has
now been dropped; but, according to the Greater
Manchester Transport Action Group, the whole scheme
would, at the rate of road building so far, have taken three
hundred years to complete. Alan Stones's article 'Liverpool
Now' (*Built Enviroment*, March 1977) provides a third
example.

Liverpool's development plans had always incorporated a substantial 'primary road networks'. However, there has never been enough finance to implement more than a small part of it . . . Last year the previously 'essential' Inner Ring Motorway scheme and the link from it to the M62 were formally abandoned. So far, 30.4ha of land has been cleared for highway use in the inner area, but only 2.7ha of this formed any part of any programmed works. The majority of the cleared highway sites are in the form of long, narrow strips that the Council has decided, rightly or wrongly, are incapable of alternative development for housing or industry, and will have to become open spaces (for which, incidentally, no funds are available.)

Insane things were done everywhere. The traffic counts showed that Arundel Street, Portsmouth, was carrying at peak hours 400 per cent of its calculated traffic capacity. It was therefore decided to widen it in order to make it capable of carrying the traffic it already was carrying. After this was done, new figures for road capacity were officially issued and they showed that in its old width it was capable of carrying what it always did carry. Now, of course, after widening, it is grossly underused.

Happily while all this has been going on, there has been something of a revolution in ideas about town planning; but hardly any of the new ideas have yet had much effect on the ground, although they have been successful in stemming the advance of the demolition and road-construction mania. The new ideas are to a large extent old ideas. There has been a realisation that many of the unquestioned assumptions of town planning were wrong, and that what happened as a matter of course before town planning was in vogue, was in many ways better than what has been designed since. Take for instance the Edwardian semi-detached. These houses have been the butt of ridicule by the 'modern' movement in architecture, yet as Nicholas Taylor points out (*The Village in the City*), they provide a more satisfactory and, indeed, sophisticated family home than anything that has been provided on any large scale in the post-war years.

Taylor cites the absurd advocacy of the famous Roehampton development, which set the fashion for highrise all over the country, in terms of even the poor having their private park. The Roehampton highrise scheme was built in three formerly private parks; but, as Taylor points out, the whole point of a private park is that it is private, and the owner and his family have the exclusive use of it. At Roehampton and other similar developments the 'parkland' is only too public and more often than not it carries notices saying 'keep off the grass', 'no ball games on the grass', etc. It was actually claimed by some architects that the provision of all this communal space would engender a communal spirit and a greater respect for public property. As everybody knows, the reverse was the case at Roehampton and in similar schemes elsewhere – the tenants resented the fact that they had nowhere of their own. Taylor's conclusion, with which I concur, is that 'Privacy is nothing to be ashamed of. It is in fact of paramount importance to most families, the five foot garden fence or wall making an incalculable gain in their happiness'.

To be specific, the theories that were held to be sacrosanct and are now emerging as mistaken are as follows:

1 The aims of rigid zoning into exclusively residential, commercial, industrial, etc., zones and the ousting of all 'non-conforming users' – resulting in longer journeys to work, an absence of plumbers and jobbing repair builders in residential areas, and excessive vandalism – and crime generally. (Because the main deterrent is casual observation. Areas which are exclusively residential tend to be empty by day and the same goes for exclusive shopping areas by night.)

2 The idea of comprehensive redevelopment as the best way of revitalising run-down areas of cities. (The word 'comprehensive' being used in quite a different sense from its use as applied to schools.)

3 The surrounding of new developments with open space. (I do not of course mean playgrounds or parks, but the useless open spaces variously called grass verges, amenity strips, or architectural landscaping – useless public space at the expense of usable private space in the form of private back gardens. And this has been widely linked with the fallacy that the minimising of private facilities and the maximising of communal ones – corridors, washing machines, etc. – all makes for an increase in communal spirit and willingness to take responsibility for communal and private property. In fact, of course, the opposite is more nearly true.

4 The theory held by municipal architects that buildings have a natural life of the order of 100 years and that after that it is uneconomic to try to prop them up. This is in bland disregard of the fact that most architects themselves actually choose to live in houses of up to three hundred years old in preference to those of their own design, and probably wisely so.

5 The idea that road widening is necessarily an improvement while road narrowing is never thought of.

6 The idea that specially built double carriageway roads with no access to neighbouring buildings can drain off not only through traffic, but local traffic, from shopping and residential streets.

7 The assumption that traffic everywhere increases automatically and inevitably at 5 per cent per year.

These ideas have common characteristics of ruthlessness, disdain for the opinion of people who are actually most likely to be directly affected, and contempt for tradition and local vernacular. They are nearly all of this century or of the very end of the nineteenth century. They are holist in spirit and they were carried out by solutioneering as opposed to problem-solving. Many can be traced to Ebenezer Howard and the garden city ideal, which itself was based on the idea that industry, all industry, was necessarily noxious and people must be enabled to live far away from it, and that cities were inherently nasty and must be made as much like the country as possible. There were good reasons for Howard's feelings. Industry *was* nasty then. But the ideas were put into practice on a large scale long after most of industry had, largely as a consequence of electric power, become much nicer, when in most cases it was better to live next to a factory than to a pub or a school.

But another powerful force behind the planning movements that have so changed our cities can be traced to none other than Karl Marx. The general acquiescence in the idea that society should be planned, and that it is either possible or sensible to plan twenty years ahead, derives from historicism. For it assumes that we know the direction in which 'society as a whole' is moving – and that we can do nothing to stop it if we do not like it.

The lame horse theory of houses, the idea that houses have a 'useful life' is not dead. The majority of Victorian houses that escaped the German bombers and the British bulldozers have gradually over the years been repaired and greatly altered inside. Bedrooms have been changed into bathrooms, dining rooms into bedrooms or garages, small rooms have been knocked into one and large rooms have been divided. Gas, electricity, internal w.c.s, copper plumbing and central heating have been installed, sometimes in one swoop but more often piecemeal, while the main brick structure has usually remained unaltered and still needs no alteration. This is the reality. But officially houses are either 'improved' or 'unimproved'; and improvement is seen, still in the light of the 'useful life' theory, as a kind of transplant that extends 'life', but only for thirty years.

So there is a new bogey, a new-improved lame horse theory, being hinted at whenever the question is raised of whether to demolish or not. We may be laying up trouble for the next generation. In thirty years' time, it is hinted, there will be the same demand for comprehensive redevelopment as there was (according to re-written history) in the '50s and '60s. It is really a sociological theory disguised as a practical matter of the structure of buildings and confused by historicism. What the bogey-man is saying is that by 2010 people will no longer be content to live in this sort of house; but it is put over in such a way as to suggest that they may all then collapse. But the sociological fact is that Coronation Street–type houses form part of a 'housing ladder'. They tend to be acquired by young couples – in the jargon: first-time buyers, who, if they prosper, move on to something more spacious. Thus the *same* people do not have to put up with this sort of house for thirty years. Furthermore should it turn out that fewer and fewer people of any sort want these houses as time goes on, then there is the obvious remedy now known as 'gradual renewal', that is gradual replacement with new, the process that obtained for centuries until comprehensive redevelopment brought it to a halt.

At least until the demise of the Callaghan government, civil servants from the Department of the Environment were touring the country inspecting General Improvement Areas, preaching this lame horse doctrine and so advocating more demolition, a policy contrary to that of their political masters.

* * *

An interesting example is provided by Frank Guy of how, in the absence of a routine of criticism, absurd practices can become widespread or practices, sensible in one context, can become fashionable and then be copied inappropriately in another. He describes the background to the prefabrication, by metal-framed sections, of post-war new schools, something that has been widely acclaimed outside the architectural profession (who know what they cost) and the teaching profession (who know what they like to teach in). A shortage of bricklayers in post-war Hertfordshire was the ostensible reason for trying to meet the need for new schools by non-traditional building methods. Standard steel-framed sections were factory-made and assembled on site. A different system known as CLASP (Consortium of Local Authorities Schools Projects – Guy's title is 'Unclasp me'), was developed by the Nottinghamshire County architects, although Nottingham

City stuck to bricks. (Guy comments drily 'The shortage of bricklayers was extremely local.') Since the buildings could be supported at intervals on jacks, they had a genuine advantage over traditionally constructed ones in mining areas where there was soil subsidence. On this Guy remarks: 'Of course it meant either that most buildings were structurally redundant and to that extent uneconomic, or that one scoured the country looking for old mines over which to site schools.' He continues 'In the lush green counties of the south (now full of bricklayers) yet another iron-frame system was born, SCOLA Mark I. Later reconnaissance having failed to reveal any old coalmines, SCOLA Mark II is now done without the frame, which introduces a doubt.' What Guy is saying with gentle derision is that rationalised traditional construction could have done the job better and cheaper, except only in the sites with subsidence. For as well as high initial costs, maintenance costs on these buildings are high and so are heating costs because of the light structure, with poor thermal insulation and low thermal capacity, and 'huge areas of glass – baking hot in summer, leaking heat like mad in winter'. The demand for huge areas of glass masked, Guy says, 'the inherent inefficiency of using a frame for a school. As long as windows were enormous one felt a frame might be necessary'. But the excessively large windows were also the result of a muddle. They were required by a daylighting standard derived mistakenly from a wartime standard for factories. It is perhaps mainly the huge windows that make the prefabricated schools less comfortable to teach in than the old ones.

Colin Ward has written recently:

There used to be a map of education authorities on the wall at the Department of Education and Science, coloured according to the various consortia of authorities with joint systems for school construction. A white patch in the middle stood out as a reproach. This was Buckinghamshire, who went on building purpose-designed schools of brick, timber, and pitched roofs, and who have at last been vindicated for their simple, durable, and cheaply-maintained buildings, which gave about 15 per cent more school for the money.

It is a moot point to what extent 'system-building' caught on because of the name. 'Systems-analysis' had been invented in the war for organising the planning and co-ordination of such things as aircraft production on a large scale and the mounting of huge military operations like the invasion of Normandy. The word suggested the latest thing and, in the atmosphere of historicism which prevailed, the latest thing was the good thing whether or not it was an improvement on the old. It is interesting that Max Nicolson in his book *The System* (sub-titled *The Misgovernment of Modern Britain*), although he is a penetrating critic of the civil service system, fell most uncritically for this building gimmick.

One of the most significant and successful achievements of the new Ministry (of Education) was to bring together a joint working party of architects, builders, teachers, educationists, and administrators to design and arrange for production of largely prefabricated new school buildings, of the highest possible standards and at the lowest possible cost. By this simple device, counter to all the conventional principles and practices of Whitehall, British school design and construction achieved a leading position in Europe.

This idea of the team that could do better than the individual, was another ill-conceived panacea that has often misguided us during the past twenty years or so. Somebody, ignorant of the way in which architects normally work and consult their clients, could imagine that a committee of all these people would produce a better result than an architect on his own. Similarly it has been imagined that a team of doctor, health visitor, nurse, midwife, social worker etc. can produce a better result than these individuals sticking to their own tasks. What is needed is that the expert, however he works, shall be subject to criticism. A team of experts is equally in need of criticism but less likely to receive it. There is the point made by Leslie Chapman (whose exposure of the Civil Service I quote from in Chapter 11) that 'if you create a management structure where ... for anything that needs to be decided there is a committee, and perhaps more than one committee, involved, you are well on the way to creating an organization where no one can ever be blamed for anything'.

Change of building techniques and materials and the consequent problems of water penetration and condensation illustrate another aspect of the importance of criticism. Take bricks for example. Until recent times all bricks were what what would now be called soft. It was entirely reasonable that the newer hard bricks should be used for heavy load-bearing in multi-storey buildings, for instance in the Portsdown Park development already mentioned. It is now realised that one of the advantages of the old soft bricks was their sponge-like quality which enabled them to absorb moisture. The hard modern bricks are impervious, and so driving rain tends to penetrate in larger quantities the unavoidable crevices in the brickwork. I am not saying that in the old days they knew better. They did not have to know. The old bricks worked well. Probably nobody ever bothered to wonder why. It is only when we come to replace them that we come to appreciate their qualities. So it is, I suggest, with all tradition. We may not be able to see any reason, there may well have been no reason as such, in a traditional practice; but this does not mean that we can abandon it with impunity. We must always expect, in changing from something that works well to something which looks as if it should work better, that there will be unforeseen snags, indeed unforeseeable ones. We have to try and see what happens. We readily see the white swans; but we must look for the black ones. This is not of course to say that tradition is good and innovation bad. We need both and we need a critical attitude to both.

Benefits which could be obtained more certainly by a direct, piecemeal, approach are sometimes obtained incidentally by holist solutioneering and retrospectively claimed to justify it. Terence Bendixson quotes from a speech in May 1973 by the then Secretary of State for the Environment:

> One of the aims of our current programme of strategic roads is to achieve environmental improvements by relieving a large number of towns and villages in this way. Of the 520 towns in England with a population over 10,000, about 100 have by-passes or high quality relief roads and by the end of the 1980s another 150 will have been completed . . .

And then, warming to his subject, He goes on:

> Some of the effects of such relief can be measured and expressed in terms of reduced levels of noise and pollution, but the main benefit is to the well-being of local inhabitants: the relief from stress through being rid of noisy, smelly, intrusive traffic which they feel should not be there.

On looking at this speech the other way round, Bendixson points out, what emerges is that by the end of the 1980s (officialese for 1990) more than half of the towns mentioned will still be *without* a by-pass. Five miles of 24-foot two-lane by-pass can be constructed for the cost of each mile of motorway. Now, if the preliminary operation had been to list the most urgent problems concerning road traffic, and if, as most of those affected would certainly have said, *the* most urgent problem was to free towns and villages of heavy through-traffic, then it might have led to an entirely different idea – abandon the motorway *network* (not necessarily abandon all motorway construction) – and make the first priority the construction of by-passes. Then probably all the 520 towns could be relieved of through traffic by 1990, with all the advantages that the Minister listed.

This solution, unlike the strategic motorway network, would not appeal to those of holist mentality and, if ever

considered in the 1960s, was doubtless dismissed as merely
tinkering with the problem. Rather late in the day, it is
now being adopted, at least in the south of England, where
the south coast motorway is being abandoned in favour of
local by-passes. I suspect that this is one instance where
ministers have managed to get the better of their
professional advisers.

It is important to note that the Minister justified the
holist solution, the strategic network, by its welcome
popular effect of relieving towns of traffic, which it will do
only incidentally. The solution is justified in other words
as compared with doing nothing rather than compared
with a plan specifically designed to relieve towns of
through-traffic. This dishonesty is a very common practice.
Objectors to holist schemes are regularly made to appear as
opposing the desirable object of improving the conditions
of the people in whatever way it may be – better housing,
better education etc., when what they are really objecting
to is the particular solution proposed which, often enough,
both fails to achieve its alleged object economically, and
gratuitously ruins a hundred perfectly good houses by the
way.

Once on the look-out for solutioneering, one finds
examples of it in surprisingly rational-seeming disguise.
The M.O.T. test for cars which are more than three years
old is, on the face of it, a rational measure for improving
road safety. However there were no official figures for
accidents due to defective vehicles before 1961 when the
test was introduced, according to Malcolm Hulke, and
now that there are, they hardly support the idea. The 2,130
accidents that occurred between 1970 and 1974 within
twenty miles of the Transport and Road Research
Laboratory (TRRL) in Berkshire were studied in detail.
Only $2\frac{1}{2}$ per cent of these could be attributed to vehicle
defects alone; and in $89\frac{1}{2}$ per cent vehicle defects played no
part. On the other hand 65 per cent were solely the fault of
road users. The TRRL reported that of 632 'impaired'
drivers, 463 were drunk, 159 tired, 87 drugged, and 26
unhappy. Obviously only a very small return could be
expected in terms of lives saved from measures to bring all

vehicles even up to 100 per cent efficiency, very small compared, for instance to 'don't drink and drive' measures.

It certainly looks as though the institution of the M.O.T. test was a piece of solutioneering, coupled perhaps with a holist prejudice against patching up old cars, the idea being to try to force them off the road and replace them with new ones. Certainly there was no previous study to indicate the extent of the problem, no precise formulation of what it was, and no monitoring of the effect. Since it was started, its range has been greatly extended and its cost increased, so obliging the non-mechanical members of the public to be the dupes of unscrupulous garages.

* * *

The threat to democracy posed by the misuse of computers has been brought to light most clearly in public inquiries associated with proposed new motorways and other major roads. The case for the road is always based by the Department of Transport on a cost–benefit analysis (C.O.B.A.) which takes into account one cost (the cost of building the road) and three benefits: the savings of time, vehicle operating costs, and accidents. As Dr John Adams points out, cash evaluation of these four elements yields a quite arbitrary cost–benefit ratio. Of the four, one (construction costs) is a hard cash element, one (vehicle operating costs) is generally insignificant, one (time saving) is highly contentious, and one (the cost of accidents) is meaningless. This last confuses 'the price that someone is prepared to pay to safeguard something he values (for example his life) with the price he would consider fair compensation for its loss'. (And the second, if the something *is* life, ties the cost–benefit analysts into logical knots when they 'try to calculate the cash compensation that ought to be paid to someone who is dead and incapable of spending it'. At that time (1976) C.O.B.A. valued a fatal accident at £44,000, a little more, Adams pointed out, than 'the damage done to the reputation of an actor' [the creator of Kojak] 'by a newspaper article which claimed that he got drunk and forgot his lines'.

Although the death and serious injury rate per passenger mile is much less on motorways than on other roads as a whole (largely because there are no pedestrians or cyclists and these two categories of road users make up 50 per cent of the serious casualties on other roads), there can be no doubt that one of the effects of building a motorway is to increase the amount of traffic in the country as a whole. Since the more traffic there is, the more accidents there are, it must follow that motorways cause accidents elsewhere. So although the casualties on a motorway itself can be expected to be low, its true costs even in accidents are not taken into account because it will cause them elsewhere. In fact what is counted as a benefit is really a cost.

This system is objectionable in two ways. First the C.O.B.A. rests on the assumption that everyone has his price. Again Adams exposed this nicely when he said:

The sincere exasperation of C.B. analysts with a man who cannot, or will not, name his price illustrates what an insidiously corrupting poison cost–benefit analysis is. It used to be a common view that people ought to hold certain things, the most valuable things, above price. The extent to which this view is less common than previously is a measure of the increased acceptance of the cost–benefit ethic. It is an ethic which debases that which is important and disregards entirely that which is supremely important.

Secondly, although C.O.B.A. is based on the analysis of only four factors, the calculation of them is extremely complicated and can be done only by a computer. And for all that the public know the statistics that form the material for these abstruse and inaccessible calculations may be gathered by the process described by Mr Denis Healey, the former Chancellor of the Exchequer, who while unfit for active service during the war, was posted to Swindon station to replace 'a drunken bombadier who was a railway checker'. Mr Healey told a newspaper interviewer that he had learnt there 'a lesson of lasting importance about statistics'. 'One of my jobs', he said, 'was to count all the service people getting *on* every train, getting *off* every train, and *off and on* again, on six platforms in the blackout.' It was an impossible job. He had to invent the numbers getting on, and off and on, and went to the ticket collector to get the numbers of those who were getting off. 'After I'd been there a fortnight I found that *he* made up his numbers too!' His comment was that he suspects that a great deal of economic planning today is based on this kind of statistics. At any rate – to return to C.O.B.A. – the figures that emerge have the status of a revelation. The Department of Transport, as the saying is, has a hot line to God. The objectors to the Department's schemes have no direct communication with God. The most they can do is to express their scepticism.

That one side of the argument in a public debate should be incomprehensible to the public negates democracy and reduces these inquiries to the status of a farce. It also means that however much expertise the Department of Transport may deploy, their calculations lack the objective status of science because, as has already been stated, that objectivity depends not on such things as the efficiency of computers, but on anybody so minded being able to check the calculations for himself. Computer scientists themselves have a saying: 'garbage in, garbage out'.

Now it happens that on two recent occasions, there have been, among the objectors to the Department of Transport's schemes, people with the necessary time and expertise to repeat the C.O.B.A. for themselves; and on these two occasions they have shown the calculations to be wrong. It has not been made very clear in the press what has been the reason for the many disruptions of the proceedings at motorway inquiries. They have been portrayed as being due to people seeking to take the law into their own hands. On the contrary, they see themselves, I think rightly, as upholders of the democratic process and the law (a view with which the Court of Appeal now seems to agree). Until the disorderly disruptions, evidence against the need for road schemes was, contrary to the Highways Act of 1959, disallowed at public inquiries. Objectors were allowed only to dispute the route. There were a number of other irregularities of procedure which John Tyme goes into in his book *Motorways Versus Democracy*. Mr John Thorn, Headmaster of Winchester College, who was marched out of one inquiry, was particularly incensed:

> The workings of our so-called democracy in this matter of roads is left to tribunals whose composition and procedures are reminiscent not of the English Common Law Courts, but of Tudor treason trials . . . Respectable, law-abiding and peace-loving citizens do not lightly behave noisily in public . . . but occasionally, just occasionally, they feel something so deeply, become so frustrated with a system which denies them power while granting them speech, that they begin non-violently to behave like rebels.

These attitudes have been abundantly justified now in retrospect by the revelation of the serious official miscalculations. Not only have the Department of Transport behaved high-handedly, but their case has been arithmetically wrong. Needlesss to say, in both cases the error was in the direction of forecasting greater benefits from their schemes than were warranted by the assumptions made. It is now apparent that the burying in concrete of what Mr Thorn described as 'one of the most beautiful square miles of stone, river, and meadow, in the whole of western Europe' (the south-eastern fringe of Winchester) might have been deemed justified in the interests of the country's economy on the basis of a computer operator's error. This surely rams home the point that theories and calculations must not be relied upon until serious public attempts have been made to refute them and have failed.

In a B.B.C. television programme (24.2.79) reviewing a series of films on post-war planning and architecture, the question arose as to who had had the power to carry through, for example, the decision to build pre-fabricated tower blocks and slabs. Was it the architects, the planners, the politicians, the construction companies? Christopher

Booker, the author of one of the films (a devastating exposure of the disasters discussed here) replied. He said he could answer the question in one word: it was the 'vision', the vision of the city of the future, something partly but not wholly derived from Le Corbusier, something not precisely spelt out and never systematically criticised. This World 3 object was the culprit.

9

Blinding with science

> Of nearly every theory it may be said that it agrees with many facts: this is one of the reasons why a theory can be said to be corroborated only if we are *unable* to find refuting facts, rather than if we *are* able to find supporting facts. Popper (P.H. 111n)

In most people's eyes, whatever may be said against science, it works. The facts of space travel, television, computers – to name just three of the spectacular products of inventions based on scientific discoveries – proves to most people's satisfaction that science is not nonsense.

But although, in performing his task of formulating theories and testing them, a scientist may need to amass data and possess the skills necessary to operate an electron microscope or to programme a computer, these skills of themselves do not make a scientist. It is possible for people who possess these skills to appear to be speaking with the voice of science when actually they are speaking with the voice of dogma. Genuine scientists, as well as those who are only skilled in the use of the tools of science, can lapse from the high discipline of scientific methods and begin to pontificate. To the general public it sounds like science and they are misled.

The difference between adopting a scientific outlook in the Popperian sense and an inductive one may sometimes seem very slight, but it is usually far-reaching in its consequences. A good example is the relationship between housing conditions, particularly overcrowding, and the intellectual performance of children at school, allegedly discovered by the authors of *From Birth to Seven* (Ronald Davie et al.), the second of the 'longitudinal' studies of all the children born in the United Kingdom in one week of

1958. The fallacy inherent in the conclusion was cleverly exposed by Tyrrell Burgess, a fellow-disciple of Popper, in *New Society* (1975). As the argument is rather subtle and as there are probably many unexposed instances of the same kind of fallacy, I propose to go into the matter in some detail.

In their book the authors had written: 'Poor housing is often mentioned as one of the contributory causes of school failure.' They then quoted the following from Professor R. N. Titmuss's introduction to the 1964 edition of R. H. Tawney's *Equality*: 'We delude ourselves if we think we can equalise the social distribution of life's chances by expanding educational opportunities, while millions of children live in slums, without baths, decent lavatories, room to explore and space to dream.' Having dropped these prestigious names the authors duly found that over the country as a whole 'the effect of overcrowding (defined as more than 1.5 persons per room) was equivalent to two or three months' retardation in reading age at age 7'. Surprisingly to them the effects of shared or absent basic amenities (hot water, indoor W.C.s, etc.) was much more – nine months retardation. By juggling the figures and taking into account family size, the retarding effect of overcrowding was brought up also to nine months. From this the authors drew their very definite conclusion: '*The results have demonstrated clearly the relationship between poor housing conditions and overcrowding on the one hand and on the other educational performance . . . at the age of seven*'.

However, what they did not mention, although they were contained within their own results, were other figures which Burgess extracted to fuel his fire. These show that, while Scotland as a whole contains the greatest percentage of children from overcrowded conditions (39.2 per cent compared with London and the South East's 13.4 per cent, and Eastern England's 6.6 per cent), it also produced considerably the best reading results: 40 per cent good readers compared with 31 per cent for each of the two areas I have singled out, and 28 per cent for Wales, which was the worst reading area although one of the least overcrowded (8.7 per cent). And Scotland was no flash in the pan. The second and equal third most crowded (Northern and North West) were second and third for the percentage of good readers. The statistics of this report admittedly do not exclude the possibility that bad home conditions *are* incompatible with good reading ability (nor, to take a frivolous example, do they exclude the possibility that boys called Robert are never good readers). It is admittedly possible that the 40 per cent of Scottish good readers came only from the 60.8 per cent of homes that were not overcrowded. In Wales, on the other hand, that assumption – that all the overcrowded children were bad readers – would still mean that 7 out of every 8 of the bad readers (63.3 out of 72 per cent of bad readers) would have come from the 91.3 per cent of the homes that were not overcrowded. In the case of an overwhelming majority of bad readers therefore, overcrowding could not have been a factor or link. Nor could there have been in their case any 'relationship between poor housing conditions and overcrowding on the one hand and on the other educational performance' as the authors had claimed. And even in Scotland at least a third (20.8 out of every 60) of 'bad' readers must have come from 'good' homes.

Clearly what the authors had done was to extract their own preconceived conclusion from the mass of data they had accumulated. They claimed that their data confirmed their theories when what they should have done was, as Burgess pointed out, to have formulated their hunches in a form of a precise theory such as 'there is a rate of overcrowding x at which y per cent of children failed to reach a "good" standard r'. This could have been tested, and on the evidence they had already accumulated would have been found to be false.

The authors, steeped in the idea that all one has to do is to look for evidence to confirm one's hunches, genuinely could not see the force of Burgess's criticism. David Donnison, then Director of the Centre for Environmental Studies, had written in the foreword to their book: 'The patterns glimpsed in the National Child Development Study are so deeply embedded in this country's economic and social structure that they cannot be greatly changed by anything

short of equally far reaching changes in that structure.'
Evidently they all had their eyes fixed in this one direction.
In replying to Burgess, they still maintained that 'to expect
schools to cope with this situation [by implication 'the
situation' was: being expected to teach reading successfully
in the face of bad home conditions] unaided by other
agencies and by improvements in social conditions is to
impose an unreasonable and impossible burden and to fly in
the face of virtually every piece of research on this topic'.

I thought an analogous case might help them and I cited
the fight against tuberculosis, a disease universally regarded
as fostered by overcrowding and other unhygienic
conditions, although when most rampant it had not only
spared many of the poor but also claimed its victims among
the well-to-do. Yet, by tackling the disease itself and its
means of spread and by early detection and treatment, it has
been possible almost to eradicate it from this country
(except in areas where it is constantly being reintroduced
from abroad) in spite of the fact that poverty and
overcrowding have not been abolished.

The holistic outlook, not very different from the
revolutionary outlook, tends to encourage the adoption of
vague ideas such as that bad social conditions are the cause
of (or a contributary cause of – it makes little difference)
failure to read. And you can easily find some facts to
confirm it – just as you could confirm the theory that
wealth is the result of winning the pools. It is again a case of
the swans. The authors were so busy counting their white
ones that they ignored the black ones that were staring them
in the face.

If they had been right in their conclusion, then the
consequence must be that it will take a very long time to
achieve any substantial improvement in reading standards –
as long as it will take to eliminate overcrowding and
provide universal basic amenities, or, if Donnison is right,
even longer – until the country's whole economic and social
structure has been changed. But what their results actually
show is that overcrowded home conditions are not a factor
in the poor achievement of many children, and that in some
areas *most* of the children who in fact perform badly are not

overcrowded. Their results therefore suggest that it may be possible to improve the achievement of all children *in spite* of continuing bad conditions. Even the dissemination among teachers and parents of this piece of knowledge alone would probably immediately help children who are at school now (whereas the Donnisons of this world cannot hope to benefit the present generation of school children). For there is abundant evidence from other sources that children's attainments closely match teachers' expectations. So long as educational sociologists tell teachers that they cannot expect good results from children from poor homes, so long will many teachers not attempt what they are told is impossible. Burgess's argument, of course, does not detract in any way from the need to improve bad housing conditions. But the case for doing this is easily made on its own account and does not require the help of a bogus educational theory.

Burgess commented on the quotation from Donnison as follows:

This kind of analysis is typical of educational sociology – particularly the conclusion that there is a 'combination' or 'cycle of deprivation' which means that you cannot change anything unless you change everything. The practical consequences of these 'findings' have undermined the search for effective solutions to grave social problems and encouraged the view that schools are helpless victims of an independent and destructive social process. Not only are the poor trapped in a cycle of deprivation, but the agencies that might help them are trapped in a cycle of impotence.

The 'findings' of some educational psychologists have had a similar undermining effect. Professor Denis Stott points out the fallacy in the assumption of 'disability-producing deficits' as explanations of poor school performance – dyslexia and hyperactivity are the best-known examples. These deficits, he says, 'have become an academic myth – a myth convenient to the college academic and the school psychologist because it ... provided them with a professional mystique . . . convenient to parents because it absolved them from the shame of having a dull or retarded child, and convenient to the teacher because it excused what looked like teaching failure'. These mythical deficits (presumably in the central nervous system) have been assumed as the only explanation of poor academic performance in children whose nervous systems are, by any other test, intact. (Winston Churchill would, by modern standards, have been 'deemed' hyperactive and a suitable case for treatment; and Einstein was so late in learning to talk, according to Jeremy Bernstein, that his parents were worried that he might be mentally deficient!)

It would not be true of course to say that all sociologists and educational psychologists think like the *Birth to Seven* authors. It just seems like it. One can hardly open a journal without catching a sociologist in the act of white-swanning. I open the *Guardian* and find Nicky Hart from the Department of Sociology of the University of Essex, listing, quite rightly, some of the many ways in which the vital statistics for social class V (unskilled workers) are throughout life markedly worse than those for class I (professional and managerial). 'These differences in life chances', Hart says, 'reflect the distribution of material advantage in Britain' and he makes it clear that he means by this that material inequality is the *cause* of these differences. One can be quite sure that it is not the *only* cause by virtue of the fact that the life expectancy of women in *each* social class is so consistently greater than that for men in the same class. Not even a male chauvinist pig could allege that women enjoy a marked 'material advantage' over men in their own class. Other factors must be involved; and there is much evidence that cultural habit is more important in this regard than material wealth. Just to take one fact to support this contention: the risk of serious respiratory disease in the first two years of life is increased by half for a child whose mother smokes and doubled if the father does also. Smoking is much more prevalent among young people in class V than in classes I and II and cannot be called material deprivation.

*   *   *

My second example of unreason masquerading as science concerns the distinguished biologist, the late C. H. Waddington, formerly Professor of Animal Genetics at Edinburgh, who at the end of his life wrote a book, published posthumously, entitled *Tools for Thought*.

In it, Professor Waddington makes a specific reference to Popper, but at the same time makes it clear that he does not begin to understand the force of Popper's ideas: 'Karl Popper argued that the real method of science is not to try to verify statements, but to disprove them. A surprising number of scientists, including very successful ones, have expressed agreement with him.' This is a mis-statement of Popper's position. Waddington omits the very first step – the hypothesis, the bold conjecture. He goes on: ' . . . suppose we have a hypothesis like "if a match is put to twigs a fire starts" . . . sometimes the fire does not start, the twigs are wet, or something; and this does not completely disprove the suggestion that matches have something to do with starting fires.' This is a case of careless and unprecise formulation. The original hypothesis is definite 'a fire starts', but in order to make Popper look silly, he changes it when he talks about disproof to 'something to do with starting fires', a different and vaguer proposition. 'The mistake made by both sets of philosophers', he goes on, ' – those who asked for verification and those who would settle for falsification – is that they demand 100 per cent certainty: and that is something we can never have in the real world.'

I can only describe this argument as silly. Waddington does not seem to have made any effort to discover what either set of philosophers is talking about. Popper, of course, has stipulated that hypotheses must be formulated clearly, and if the hypothesis is so wide though clear as 'a lighted match will always ignite a bunch of twigs', then one failure does, quite properly, falsify it. One then tries again, perhaps specifying the degree of dryness and thickness of the twigs, type of wood used, the absence of draught, temperature of the air, etc. One pursues this until one is unable to refute it. That is all that Popper is saying. Now Waddington goes on to give, as examples of how silly the philosophers are, that when 'Mendel discovered the laws of heredity he was not trying to disprove them'. This is of course true; but what are now known as the Mendelian laws were the bold conjectures (the step that Waddinton omitted from the process) which invited refutation. As it happens the theory has withstood all attempts to refute it and so is generally accepted.

In his introduction to the book, Waddington goes more seriously astray through not having made an effort to understand Popper's theory of the growth of knowledge and the function of social science. He starts off well enough: 'We have been trained to think, or have accepted as commonsense, that what goes on around us can usually be understood as some set of simple causal sequences in which, for instance, a causes b and b then causes c, then c causes d and so on. This is only good enough when a causes b but has very little other effect on anything else, and similarly the overwhelmingly most important effect of b is to cause c. Many of our own individual actions still have this character.' So far so good. But, 'The change which has occurred, or is occurring now, is that the effects of human society on their surroundings are now so powerful that it is no longer adequate to concentrate on the primary effects and neglect all secondary influences.' And later: 'No powerful action can be expected to have only one consequence, confined to the thing it was primarily directed at.' But it never could. Clearly he has never considered the house-buying example (page 10). a practically never does nor did cause only b. The upshot of Waddington's argument is that things are now so complicated that we must use the new 'powerful' tools of systems-analysis allied with the inevitable computer.

The conclusion is wrong and if put into effect would be disastrous because it ignores the difference between human society and complex combinations of such things as industrial processes. For the latter systems-analysis is highly successful. The technique was evolved during the second world war and was successful then, even though it involved manipulating human beings, because in the circumstances of war their individual aspirations could be ignored. The purpose of the whole enterprise was to win battles. But

cities and nations have no purpose in this sense and the
individual aspirations of their citizens cannot be ignored. It
would be a centralising of power not just in human hands
but in the computer's hands, and, as has been said before,
although it is easy to centralise power it cannot be wisely
wielded, the reason being that the computer cannot be
informed of all that knowedge in all those individual minds
which is essential for the wise wielding of power.

Any attempt to do this would be up against the same
objections as are being rightly made now against C.O.B.A.
for the motorways. The authorities would be calling on a
private line to God. It would be an attempt to answer
criticism with complexity.

Rupert Crawshay-Williams has told of the setting up of
the Metalogical Society in 1949 by Professor A. J. Ayer,
with the object of getting philosophers and scientists
together. He said that the eventual fading out of the society
was in part due to the fact that the scientists tended not to
recognise as their own the aims and methods which the
philosophers attributed to them and this was despite the
fact, he says, that 'they certainly accepted Karl Popper's
famous denial of the traditional theory that scientific
method uses induction'. He went on that 'The philosophers
(including Popper) assumed that the task of science was to
discover . . . "absolute-all" statements.' And he gives an
example of this as 'metals expand when heated' and later
mentions, to refute this statement, the new welded railway
lines which do not expand when heated. This incredible
muddle of imprecision is strongly reminiscent of what I
have just quoted from Waddington; and one cannot help
wondering whether he was the scientists' spokesman. The
statement 'metals expand when heated', with no mention of
conditions, is like Waddington's 'something to do with
starting fires'.

It is in a way typical of what has gone wrong that it
should be thought that systems-analysis is the answer. Here
is something successful in war but not directly applicable to
peacetime human problems. On the other hand war-time
lessons of universal applicability have been ignored.
Professor R. V. Jones describes how it was proposed that

our heavy bombers should be fitted with equipment to prevent losses from icing-up; but the proposal was dropped when it was realised that more bombers would be needed to make up the loads lost by the weight of the de-icing equipment and that more bombers sent out would mean more shot down. It was calculated that the extra number lost to enemy action would be significantly greater than the number that could possibly be saved by prevention of icing. The fitting of the equipment would have increased casualties rather than saved them. (Just as motorways cause more casualties than they save.) Professor Jones commented: 'This is an example of a phenomenon where an action can have the opposite effect from that intended, and a lesson always to be borne in mind by politicians and administrators.' Jones was one who did not suffer from tunnel-vision but, as we have seen, his lesson has not always been borne in mind.

The attraction of magic machinery and the over-emphasis on the large scale has obscured another war-time lesson pointed out by R. V. Jones.

The station commander at Tangmere during the flying-bomb assault had asked one squadron commander how he succeeded in getting twice as much work out of his squadron as did the other two. The answer was that this particular squadron was organised on the old system that had operated throughout the Battle of Britain. Each pilot had his own aircraft which was serviced by a devoted ground crew who regarded themselves as part of a team with the pilot. His victories were their victories. The system was extravagant in ground crews; and one of the earliest results of 'Operational Research' was to show that substantial savings could be made by changing to a kind of central garage system into which each aircraft was sent after each operation and from which each pilot could draw a serviced aircraft. The other two squadrons at Tangmere had changed to the new system. There were a number of snags to it, Jones recalls, but the main one was the loss of the team spirit which in the old individual crew system 'somehow drew substantially more work' out of the ground crew when emergencies cropped up. 'Since this is rarely quantifiable', Jones comments, 'it is usually not taken into account by any plan to improve administrative efficiency.' Computers can only compute measurable quantities. Inevitably they leave out of account what is not measurable. Our science may thus blind us to what is not measurable but not necessarily unimportant.

* * *

On the whole, in my own profession of medicine, we have I think managed to avoid the main conceptual mistakes I have outlined because our chickens usually come home to roost rather fast, a situation that is unlike that in, for example, the civil service where the authors of an idea have usually retired or moved elsewhere by the time the effect of their actions has become apparent. In particular we are from the start taught to regard as a vice the special form of solutioneering open to us (and which we are constantly tempted by patients to indulge in), that is embarking on treatment before making a diagnosis. Once led into that trap, one is liable to find oneself unable to distinguish between the unintended effects of treatment and the unidentified disease. This again tempts one to indulge in adjustments to the treatment in a manner analogous to Popper's unplanned planning.

To doctors the making of a diagnosis is always tentative, it is a hypothesis which is open to refutation and if refuted must be changed. From the very start of our careers, we cannot help realising that nothing is certain. We can never be absolutely sure of the outcome of any treatment or operation. This fact gives rise to great difficulty with the public, who expect certainty and are always pressing doctors to commit themselves and wanting a second or third opinion if certainty is not forthcoming. Unwillingly we are often forced to reveal our conjectures, such as that the possibility of malignancy must be excluded. (i.e. *One* hypothesis is that this is a case of malignant disease and we will do tests with the object of refuting that theory.) But inevitably the patient's relatives will get the message that the doctors think it *is* cancer. The tests whose 'results' are awaited with so much eagerness by patients and their relatives and received with so much disappointment when 'negative', are again attempted refutations.

A British doctor sees his immediate diagnostic task as one of excluding serious, that is potentially lethal or chronically disabling, illness rather than of answering the question 'what is it?', a question which need not be pursued at all if the symptoms rapidly subside. This Popperian, but traditional, approach contrasts with American practice which tends to aim exhaustively for certainty. I think this philosophical difference accounts to a large extent for the fact that we are able to afford a medical service which, for all its faults and gaps, is broadly comprehensive, while the Americans in spite of their wealth cannot.

The British doctor on the basis of a few simple questions, answers, and observations, can in most cases make a provisional diagnosis of this excluding sort and decide either on treatment or on a course of wait and see. Because there is no financial transaction, he can see the patient as often as necessary to check on his original diagnosis and if need be change it, in what may be a series of very brief consultations. If the patient had to pay for each attendance, he would expect more time and more tangible action from the doctor.

The American doctor, aiming at certainty, is always confronted by a patient who wants his money's worth. He has to start with an impressive battery of expensive tests employing the latest technology. The difference of approach is well illustrated by the experience of a friend of mine who was taken ill, with what turned out to be infective hepatitis (jaundice), while on a professional visit to the United States. Before being allowed to see a doctor, he was subjected to the routine battery of tests which, incidentally, did not include either a test of liver function or any examination of the urine. Simply looking at the colour of the urine, without any chemical test, would at least have suggested the diagnosis even if it did not clinch it. Only after all this was he seen by the doctor, who was about to say that, as all the tests were normal, the diagnosis by process of elimination was influenza, when for the first time he looked at the patient and saw that his eyes were yellow. In this country the doctor would have looked first and no tests would have been necessary except as base lines for measuring subsequent progress.

Something of the American attitude does sometimes obtain in British hospitals, especially in the out-patient departments, where there are no arrangements for patients to be seen frequently and briefly. Doctors there often feel themselves under an obligation to exclude every possibility (to aim for certainty). There is a definite tendency for over-investigation in the form of the ordering of expensive and sometimes (for the patient) unpleasant tests which time may well show to be unnecessary. 'The most valuable diagnostic instrument', a wise doctor remarked, 'is the passage of time.'

But so far as treatment is concerned, medical practice is only now becoming rational. Dr John Todd has rightly written that 'the supreme medical error throughout the ages has been to devise treatment from theory and deduce that it *must* be effective. Until very recently virtually no one compared patients who were given some remedy with those who were not'. And even recent long-term theorising has been suspect. I am thinking particularly about diet, where I believe medical advice has been wrong. A particular example was the recommendation in 1950 of the British Medical Association Committee on Nutrition. I believe the doctors concerned were blinded by their own science. Dietitians have been mesmerised by the analysis of food. So long as sufficient proteins, vitamins, etc. are contained in the food eaten, it has been assumed not to matter how these elements are combined. This was the theory by which they were guided, and they seem not to have looked for contrary evidence, nor even realised the magnitude of the assumption they were making.

They realised that the war-time 'national' flour contained nutrients which would be lost if white flour were once more to be the standard; but their opinion was (probably rightly) that these lost elements could be made up because they occurred in sufficient abundance in other foods. They did not look for evidence that the change might nevertheless be for the worse although this was readily available to them in the form of the vital statistics. These showed that there had been a halt during the war years to the previously rapid increase of such diseases as coronary heart disease and diabetes. They did not ask themselves how this could have happened during a period when living conditions as a whole had deteriorated. Their mistake, if as I believe it was a mistake, has been a very costly one in terms of the nation's health.

It has also caused an enormous waste of patients' and doctors' time and unnecessary anxiety. Children and young people frequently suffer from recurrent attacks of abdominal pain. It is usually due to constipation – not to complete blockage but to hard stools which are difficult to propel through the gut. Parents tend to jump to the conclusion that this is appendicitis; and it is right to bear this possibility in mind. Sometimes the differential diagnosis is difficult and the child has to be admitted to hospital for observation. But these attacks are usually relieved over a few weeks by a change to a diet that contains more indigestible fibrous residue.

No importance has been allowed in conventional dietary theory to whether the body has to extract the essential elements from the diet or whether the extraction has taken place before in mill or refinery. Richard Wilkinson has demonstrated that the steadily worsening mortality of men in social classes IV and V relative to classes I and II is associated with differences in diet and not much else. There is no evidence at all that shortage of vitamins or trace elements are causing the deaths of the poor, and they are certainly getting enough calories (often too many) and proteins in their sugar and chips diet (a diet for a nation with ill-fitting teeth, Aneurin Bevan called it). But they are consuming their essentials of nutrition in such a way as to rot their teeth, ulcerate their guts, and clog up their arteries and veins. It is not surprising that excessive concentration matters. The only element that we consume from the air we breath is oxygen, the other components are simply breathed in and out again. Yet everybody knows that breathing pure oxygen is quite rapidly fatal. Unfortunately, eating nearly pure carbohydrates is only slowly fatal – after from thirty to sixty years usually, and it has taken us proportionately long to learn the lesson.

Surgeon Captain Cleave has been a pioneer in refuting the conventional medical theories in these matters. He first showed that constipation was due to an over-refined diet and then refuted the orthodox theory that varicose veins, piles, and peptic ulcers were of hereditary origin (or emotional in the latter case) and put forward his own bold conjecture that the first two were the consequences of chronic constipation, but all three due to the same unnatural diet. Gradually these views are becoming acceptable to a conservative profession. Meanwhile Cleave (together with Burkitt) has moved on to an even bolder conjecture that almost the whole range of 'diseases of civilisation' including coronary artery disease, the cause of so many deaths in middle-aged men, is a result of the excessive consumption of refined carbohydrates, i.e. sugar, white flour and polished rice.

This theory is of course impossible to prove. It is also difficult to refute. The same can be said for some of the orthodox theories. In such circumstances, in the absence of hard evidence, it is rational to act on whatever seems the best theory. Doctors in general have been inhibited from accepting the Cleave–Burkitt theory because of this persisting belief that theories can be *confirmed* and that one should not act on them until they have been.

For my part I regard the present generally accepted theory that a high consumption of saturated fats is the principle *dietary* cause of coronary artery disease as rendered unlikely, if not disproved, by the fact that a hundred years ago, when as far as we know coronary artery disease was uncommon, the average consumption of saturated fat was as high as it is now, while poly-unsaturated fats played a negligible part in the diet of this country until after coronary heart disease began to be common. (This is not to deny that a poly-unsaturated fat diet may be a good *treatment* for those who already have the disease.) In the absence of definite refutations therefore I opt for and act on Cleave's theory and believe in wholemeal bread, plenty of root vegetables, and a minimum of sugar, indeed a minimum of extracted foods, e.g. whole orange rather than orange juice.

* * *

Finally I turn to a medical scientist whose work, while it has had little effect on the medical profession, has to a considerable extent misled the public.

It is well known that the statistical researches of Sir Arthur Bradford-Hill and Sir Richard Doll have made a strong case for the theory that something to do with cigarette smoking is the cause of most cases of lung cancer or carcinoma of the bronchus. It is important from the point of view of Popperian theory to note that when they embarked on their research they expected to find confirmation of their hunch that diesel fumes were the primary cause of the recent alarming increase in this disease. But the figures they amassed were not compatible with that possibility. That theory was conclusively refuted. They found that although there were some anomalies, on the whole the incidence of the disease was such that the possibility of getting it was roughly proportional to the number of cigarettes smoked. This does not, of course, prove a causal relationship. It remains a hypothesis. But P. R. Burch, Professor of Medical Physics at the University of Leeds, has obtained a considerable amount of publicity for his alternative theory that lung cancer is hereditary, that the same people have both a hereditary tendency to smoke cigarettes and to suffer from the disease. His theory is supported by rather complicated mathematical analysis in which the incidence of onset of hereditary disease of the kind he postulates is matched with the actual incidence of lung cancer. I do not pretend fully to understand his method. But just as I would criticise an architect whose buildings did not keep out the rain, although I myself could not design a satisfactory house, so I criticise Professor Burch because his theory is refuted by the facts, even though I do not fully understand how he supports his theory. It is the swans again.

The statistics show that the incidence of carcinoma of the

lung in 34,000 doctors who were followed from 1953 to 1965 was considerably lower than the incidence in the general population at the beginning of the study in 1953 and that in the twelve years of the survey it had fallen further, while the incidence in the same age range of the general population had risen. In the same period the consumption of cigarettes by the doctors had roughly halved while the change in consumption over the country as a whole was insignificantly small (Doll, 1972). These facts are simply not compatible with the cause being entirely hereditary unless doctors are considered to belong to an alien race.

Professor Burch has sought to get over part of this difficulty by the hypothesis that 'those who gave up were a self-selected group who were less addicted to smoking: it might be that few of them were genetically pre-disposed to lung cancer'. But Professor Doll had anticipated this suggestion some years previously. He had said (1967): 'If those who stop do so because they lack a genetic factor which causes both a strong desire to smoke and a predisposition to the disease, the fact that they stop will serve only to concentrate the incidence in those who continue, and will do nothing to alter the incidence in the whole group of people who were smoking originally.'

This completely refutes Burch's theory and in so doing must be considered to amount to a severe test survived by the smoking causation theory.

* * *

I do not at all mean to discredit the genuine scientific work carried out by any one of the people mentioned in this chapter. We all succumb to the temptation to preach; and my only point in selecting these examples is to demonstrate that the most illustrious can err and so to emphasise that the most humble have the right, indeed the duty, to point out mistakes and muddled thinking, whoever may be the perpetrators.

Most of the lapses from science made by scientists are cases of white-swanning, they result from the failure to realise the truth of Popper's remark quoted at the beginning of this chapter: 'Of nearly every theory it may be said that it agrees with many facts; this is one of the reasons why a theory can be said to be corroborated only if we are unable to find refuting facts, rather than if we are able to find supporting facts.' In other words it is not enough that there is a lot to say in favour of a particular scheme or theory; what matters is that there shall *not* be a lot to be said against it.

10

Some one had blunder'd

In this chapter I give details from four different fields to justify the contention made in the introduction that the philosophical errors listed there have been at the root of disasters of many kinds.

The reorganisation of the National Health Service was typical of what I have called solutioneering, a far-reaching change undertaken with only vague and untestable objectives, such as the general improvement of the efficiency of the service, and without any built-in assessment of whether those objectives were being attained. Before reorganisation there was a genuine problem created by the lack of suitable accommodation for disabled people who, while no longer in need of the facilities of a hospital, were not able to manage in an ordinary home. The Regional Hospital Boards had no power and no money to build the hostels needed. The local authorities had both, but gave the hostels a very low priority. The result was that costly hospital beds were clogged by people who had no need of their expensive facilities. It would clearly have been ridiculously easy to devise an ad hoc solution to this problem. It could have been made a duty for local authorities to provide hostels; Regional Hospital Boards could have been given the money and the duty to use it for this purpose; or special authorities could have been set up with the one function of filling this gap.

Yet the need to solve this problem was the only concrete example that Sir George Godber, then the Chief Medical Officer to the Department of Health and Social Security, gave in an hour long lecture to NHS staffs in Portsmouth to justify the enormous upheaval that his Department were advising the government to embark on. The clean sweep that was carried out made it impossible to predict the consequences except that the administration of the new service would be enormously more costly than the old. The estimate was that initially administration would cost an additional £56,000,000 annually – a classic example of Heller's quip about estimating, or rather underestimating! (see page 3).

The irony is that the new Regional Health Authorities have found themselves in the same position as the old local authority health departments. They have the power and the money to build hostels, but they have what they see as far more pressing calls on their necessarily limited funds. In other words the whole huge upheaval has failed to solve the one concrete problem that its architects realised as needing to be solved, while the problem itself is more severe now than it was then. It is a fact that, through lack of suitable accommodation outside, men are being sent to prison.

It is by no means only governments and nationalised undertakings that behave irrationally. In 1972 I was intrigued by reading an advertisment for the then new Jaguar XJ12 car, which confirmed what I had previously read in motoring correspondents' gossip that this car priced at about £3,500 could immediately be resold on the open market for about £5,000. The advertisement took pride in this fact and mentioned that customers were being asked to sign an undertaking that they would not resell.

I was so puzzled as to what could be the reason for this apparent eagerness to subsidise their customers to the tune of some £1,500 a time that I wrote to the Managing Director, who was good enough to reply. I pointed out that if the firm were to charge £5,000 and make a profit of £1,500 on each car while the going was good, this profit could be ploughed back into the business in order to increase production and make them more able to compete, for example, with Mercedes. We carried on quite an exchange of letters. The gist of his answers was that the high market price was the consequence of the large demand for a car in very short supply. When, as they hoped it soon would, supply increased, the market price must fall. If, therefore, they charged £5,000 now, they might well soon find that they would have to reduce the price in order to maintain demand. 'There is no doubt that in these circumstances we should be accused of blackmail.' I replied that I thought their potential critics were under the same delusion as themselves, that the price charged must be related to current costs of production. If they were to reduce their price in the future, they would, on the contrary, be praised for their efficiency in cutting their costs. Indeed they would be able to make the announcement of a reduction of price, proudly, in these terms – of 'being able' to reduce it.

The letter repeatedly talked of looking forward to what they called a 'free market situation'. In fact they seemed almost to be planning for, if not looking forward to, the day when their cars would be a drag on the market. It seemed, as I said to them, as though they had never heard of the law of supply and demand or imagined that it had been superseded. By all means give the customer the feeling that he was getting a good buy, by pricing the car a few hundred pounds initially below the market price; but £1,500 below seemed beyond all sense.

It seemed that they were so flattered at being told that their product was exceptionally good value for the money, that they lost sight of what should have been their problem, namely how to do the best for their employees, shareholders, and the country as a whole, without disregarding the interests of their customers. Had they been manufacturing a vehicle for invalids one could have defended their attitude; but, as I told them, their potential customers would seem to be among the last to deserve charity.

The same situation pertains now in regard to Land Rovers and Range Rovers which are under-priced in relation to the market. The consequence is the encouragement of quasi-criminal organisations which divert vehicles to those who are prepared to pay up to £2,000 above the market price but are not prepared to wait. The evil of the system is not only that profits that should go to the manufacturers (publicly-owned) go to the racketeers but that the firm's employees see these people pocketing far more money than they themselves can ever hope to earn by productive work.

* * *

The high charges that we all have to pay for electricity – charges which have led to great hardship for many who depend on electricity for winter warmth – are higher than they would be if we were not carrying in this country an excess of generating capacity.

The amount of generating output capacity required is governed by the simultaneous maximum demand, S.M.D. In order to allow a margin of safety for breakdowns etc., the aim is to have output capacity 20 per cent in excess of the S.M.D. However, in 1976 there was an excess capacity of 55 per cent (i.e. 35 per cent above the target) and this is likely to increase for a number of years as the S.M.D. is rising more slowly than the output. As it takes from five to ten years from ordering a new station to bringing it on line, this degree of over-estimation might seem excusable; and it has in fact been blamed on the unexpectedly low rate of economic growth, on the oil crisis, and on the advent of natural gas. However the Open University's Energy Research Group have convincingly shown that these excuses will not do and that the errors date from the early 1960s before any of these factors was operative. The mistakes were in fact examples of trendism, of assuming that an observed trend is a kind of law and that it will go on indefinitely. In this case there was clear evidence that it was not doing so.

The S.M.D. for electricity grew between 1923 and 1950 roughly exponentially, that is to say (cf. page 98) the growth could be expressed as a constant percentage (about $5\frac{1}{2}$ per cent) of the previous year's demand. But the figures show that since 1960 demand has grown only linearly, and since 1970 even less rapidly than that. Yet the forecasters continued to estimate an exponential growth. The Energy Research Group say:

It would be unreasonable to expect a forecaster in 1954 to anticipate a change from exponential to linear growth in 1960 . . . it would require a very sharp forecaster to have spotted the turnover by 1960 (when forecasts for 1966–68 were being made). However, by 1964 the trend is obvious, and it requires a very blinkered forecaster to persist in using an exponential projection from 1964 to 1974 when the trend is clearly not exponential . . . The only reasonable conclusion is that the industry planners did not want to see a trend away from exponential growth – so they didn't.

Their conclusion is borne out by this quotation from electricity forecast documents:

From 1954/55 to 1962/63 total sales expanded at the rate of 11.6 per cent per annum, but during the subsequent period 1972/73 the annual growth rate fell to 6.3 per cent and between 1972/73 and 1974/75 the average growth rate was only 2.1 per cent. (Electricity Council 1975).

These are the words of somebody who insisted on seeing a straight line as something that perversely kept on deviating from a curve.

And there were those who were not blinkered. In his diaries, Richard Crossman describes the agonies that ministers went through in meeting after meeting during the financial crisis of 1968 in deciding what cuts to make in public spending in order to placate the International Monetary Fund. He mentions a report by the Brookings Institute which recommended big cuts in what they believed was the gross over-investment programme of the Central Electricity Generating Board. Crossman commented: 'Even a fractional slow-down of these programmes could . . . avoid any cuts in the social services.' But it was not to be. The axe fell, as it did in the repeat performance in the middle 1970s and again in 1979, mainly on social expenditure.

A number of plausible explanations were advanced for the failure of the electricity industry to predict demand; but 'By and large', say the Energy Research Group, 'these explanations start from the presumption that the forecast was actually correct and that the world behaved perversely.'

The capital costs of power stations account for about 25 per cent of current electricity generating costs. If these are about 35 per cent too high through over-investment, it means that our charges are about 8¾ per cent too high. By 1980 the corresponding figures are likely to be 38 per cent and 9½ per cent. If it had not been for the very large recent disproportionate rise in fuel costs the forecasters' errors would have been even more apparent. In that event the capital costs would have formed a much larger proportion of the whole and, therefore, a miscalculation of them would have had a greater effect on the consumer charges.

Unfortunately the effects of the miscalculation are not confined to the price the consumer has to pay. The over-capacity threatens the electrical engineering industry. For the obvious remedy to the situation is to order no more power stations until the S.M.D. approaches the output capacity and this may not occur for many years as the gap is probably widening. To do this would be to kill an industry which will be needed again sometime in the future. Already the government has been forced, in order to save the industry, to order a power station which is not in fact needed. So far-reaching are the effects of a naive belief in trends.

In the early months of 1979, in spite of the excessive surplus of generating capacity, we were brought to the brink of a large-scale electricity shut-down for rather absurd reasons. A period of unusually cold weather resulted in both the National Coal Board's stockpiles and the C.E.G.B.'s own coal stocks being frozen (literally) so that they could not be moved to the power stations. There were days when there was a margin of only 2 per cent – 45,000 megawatts of *available* capacity facing 44,000 MW of demand. A C.E.G.B. statement (reported in the *Guardian* – 1 February 1979) took the opportunity to hit back at those who had criticised them. The narrow escape from disaster, they insisted, showed that the country 'cannot run on smaller generating margins'.

In replying to this statement, Professor J. W. Jeffery was provoked to derision. 'Obviously we must build more power stations', he said in a letter to the *Guardian*, 'but supposing *their* coal stocks get frozen up also?' If just some of the heat that went to warm the rivers and the sea were used instead to keep the coal heaps warm, he pointed out, we should have had 32 per cent excess capacity in the coldest spell for many years. 'They plan for 20 per cent overcapacity, achieve 32 per cent (50 per cent if you count the 'mothballed' stations) and then, with enough waste heat available to warm a large proportion of the nation's houses . . . get to the edge of breakdown because their coal stocks are frozen solid.'

Had the mental attitude of the C.E.G.B. been one of facing problems rather than solutioneering, it is inconceivable that they would have come up with the answer they did. Faced with the problem of preventing their huge surplus of plant from being immobilized by frost, they could hardly have proposed to solve it by looking towards a still larger surplus.

* * *

As a final example of irrationality in high places, I cite what was, in terms of money and of Britain's earning ability as well as our reputation as a technological nation, the most expensive of all blunders. This was the series of misjudgements which led to the probably irretrievable decline of our aerospace industry. It was comprehensible, I think, only in terms of the philosophical errors that this book is concerned with. No band of conspiratorial saboteurs could have hoped to have destroyed so much.

In the many discussions that took place after the end of the second world war regarding Britain's economic future, it was frequently stated, and I think generally agreed, that this country should, so far as a choice was possible, put its eggs into the aircraft as opposed to the car industry, because of our comparatively poor raw material resources and our comparatively high resources of human skill and ingenuity.

By 1951 it appeared that we were well on our way to capturing a good share of the world market for aircraft. 'The Comet I . . . was well on the way to entering service as the world's first pure-jet commercial transport, while the Viscount was in production at Weybridge as the first turboprop commercial airliner. At Filton, Bristol were assembling the prototype Britannia long-range turboprop aircraft.' A series of, at the time unexplained, crashes grounded the Comet I; but this need not have been the end of Britain's hopes.

Derek Wood in his book, quoted above, *Project Cancelled*, describes in detail the events leading to the cancellation of a whole series of promising aeronautical projects on which a total of £1,000 million at 1974 prices had been spent. He does not suggest that all should have been allowed to go on; but he does suggest that a substantial number had, at the time of their cancellation, good commercial prospects, far better in fact, than Concorde ever had. I shall touch on just two of these – the Vickers VC7 airliner and the Fairey FD2 supersonic fighter project.

In 1949, in accordance with a suggestion from the Air Ministry, the Fairey company embarked on a design for a transonic research aircraft. They decided to design it so that, if successful, it could be developed into a fighter. The plane, the Fairey Delta, turned out to be much faster than anybody outside the design team ever expected. It caused amazement when, in March 1956, it broke the (American held) airspeed record of 822 mph by more than 300 mph, setting a new record of 1132 mph.

Fairey at once set their sights on a development of this aircraft, called FD2, to meet the Air Ministry's specification, OR329/F.155T, which called for a two-seater fighter capable of climbing to 60,000 feet and achieving Mach 2 (twice the speed of sound) in six minutes. Owing to regulations about supersonic flying over Britain, Fairey came to an agreement with the French firm Dassault to use their airfield in France for development flying. The FD2 made 47 such flights in October and November 1956. On 1st April 1957, Fairey were tipped off by the Ministry of Supply, Wood says, that their FD2 was favourite for the F.155T contract. Three days later Mr Duncan Sandys announced in the Commons that development of all high performance piloted aircraft was to cease and that we were to rely henceforth on rocket-propelled missiles.

Dassault were developing a similar design to the Fairey

Delta. The silhouettes of the two machines were almost identical. The fact of Fairey's speed record probably influenced the French government to give the development contract to Dassault; and the success of the FD2's proving flights from the French airfield undoubtedly confirmed Dassault's confidence in their own design, which went into production as the Mirage. Twelve hundred machines of this type were subsequently sold all over the world. The FD2 never flew again. Dassault is said to have told a British aviation chief later that 'if it were not for the clumsy way you tackle things in Britain, you could have made the Mirage yourselves'.

The first of the four-jet 'V' Bombers, the Vickers Valiant, flew in 1951. The Ministry of Supply suggested to Vickers that they should develop a transport version for the R.A.F. Work on it, the V1000, began in October 1952 to a Ministry of Supply specification. The design was such that it could be easily modified to a civil airliner, to be called the VC7. In 1955 the R.A.F. began to have cold feet. Under Treasury pressure they moved towards cancellation, saying there was no longer requirement for an all-jet transport. On the civil side B.O.A.C. (British Overseas Airways Corporation), the only potential British customers, had as long ago as 1949 ordered the Britannia. This turboprop airliner was potentially more economical than a pure jet but much slower. Before this was even in service B.O.A.C. ordered 60 of its rather faster successor type (which, in fact, never materialised) still on the drawing board. While B.O.A.C. dithered about the VC7, the President of Trans Canada Airlines flew to Britain specially to implore the Minister of Supply (Mr Reginald Maudling), to go on with the VC7 because he wanted it for his airline. This action seemed to prompt Sir Miles Thomas, the head of B.O.A.C., to say that he would not buy it. The upshot was an announcement by Mr Maudling on the 11th November 1955 that both the military V1000 and the civil VC7 were cancelled, the latter because 'BOAC have no requirement for it, as the aircraft they already have on order will fully meet their needs until well into the 1960s'. Nearly £4,000,000 of public money had been spent on the V1000. Only one year later, on the 24th October 1956, the Minister of Transport and Civil Aviation announced that the government had approved the purchase by B.O.A.C. of fifteen American Boeing 707s at a cost of £44,000,000. The VC7 could have been in *nonstop* Atlantic service by 1959. The Boeing 707s, which started in service in August *1959*, had at that time to make one stop en route. Mr Maudling afterwards said, perhaps with some truth, that there was nothing that he could have done. Neither the R.A.F. nor the B.O.A.C. were prepared to place an order. Certainly B.O.A.C. had a lot to answer for. Nationalisation does not seem to ensure that decisions are taken in the national interest.

There is a strong possibility that behind these muddles there lurked the mistaken quest for certainty. Ministers, airline bosses, and air marshals were discouraged by such things as the disasters to the first Comets and the inability of prototypes of other designs to meet the requirements at once. For example, at the time of its cancellation, the Rolls Royce engines for the VC7 could not take the plane nonstop across the Atlantic, but 'stretched' versions of the engines were being developed (and B.O.A.C. knew about this); and these more powerful engines were, in fact, fitted to the Boeings which B.O.A.C. subsequently purchased. There lurked in the heads of the people who took these decisions the idea that, if things were not right straight off, there was something *radically* wrong with the design. Better then wait until the Americans had got something *proven* to offer and then buy that. They failed to appreciate the trial and error nature of aircraft design, as of everything else.

Wood tends to blame the technical ignorance of ministers and civil servants for these disasters. I think one must blame their failure to realise that a good decision, a reasonable plan, can only emerge from a situation of criticism. It may be objected that in the case of a fighter aircraft secrecy is essential. Certainly it would have been difficult to arrange a fully public discussion. But Professor R. V. Jones has described how, even at the height of the war, he was allowed by Churchill to argue his case, that rockets were being developed at Peenemunde, against the establishment view. Even if a discussion cannot be fully public it is much better to allow discussion among those who are privy to the secret than no discussion at all. The fact that someone in the Ministry of Supply was able to tell the Fairey company to expect the go-ahead on the FD2 when three days later the Minister announced a cancellation of all such projects, shows that the decision was taken in extreme secrecy, excluding officials who knew about the existence of the project.

In the case of the VC7 and of the other airliner plans that were cancelled, discussion and criticism could have been fully public. What was lacking was the institution whereby these cancellation decisions could only be taken in the framework of a fully argued discussion. What was wanted was something like the institution of listed building consent, whereby no sudden decision can be taken to pull down a listed building but procedures exist whereby the case for not pulling it down can be forcefully argued.

Popper's dictum, that we must so organise things that even incompetent rulers cannot do too much damage, is the point. It is no good arguing that we must have better ministers or better civil servants. Here were two ministers whose other actions have shown that they were well above the average level of competence. The same could be said of Mr Roy Jenkins and Mr Wilson who, later on, cancelled Britain's TSR2 in favour of the American F.111, which was in an early stage of development and which later got bogged down as badly if not worse than the TSR2, in technical difficulties and escalating costs, so that the British order for that, too, was eventually cancelled. It was the lack of proper institutional safeguards for criticism that enabled these very competent ministers to deal deathblows to the whole industry and thereby wound the whole economy.

In a final example, not of a blunder committed but of one towards which we may be heading, I want to emphasise that criticism of large national projects needs to be wide-ranging. The current nuclear energy controversy, as publicly argued at present, turns mostly on the questions of environmental hazards and costs. But a recent study has shown how employment prospects are also affected. Dr D. Elliott of the Open University has compared likely employment in the energy-producing industries by the year 2000 in the event of a nuclear 'strategy' with that under a 'fairly moderate non-nuclear programme'. The latter would combine conservation technologies – that is straightforward energy-conserving measures as well as C.H.P. (page 103), and heat pumps – with a wide range of renewable energy technologies: solar, wind, wave, and tidal power, biosynthesis and geothermal energy. Elliott draws on official documents for his estimates of what is feasible, what the cost would be, and the likely employment. His conclusion is that the nuclear programme would create about 660,000 person-years of employment up to AD 2000 and would cost about £35,000 million. The non-nuclear programme would make available about the same amount of energy at a cost of about £21,200 million and create about 1,520,000 person-years of work in the same period. It seems likely that we lack the proper institution for the taking of this vital decision so that the various experts can criticise each others' views in public.

11

Democracy in action

Institutions are like fortresses. They must be well designed *and* properly manned.

Popper: P.H., 66

Our political life is still to a large extent on the wrong track to which Plato switched it more than two thousand years ago. Questions like proportional representation, how party leaders should be appointed or elected, and how parliamentary candidates should be selected – all these are questions of who should rule, while the question is largely neglected as to how should these representatives once chosen, by whatever means, be controlled, and how shall the will of the governed be brought to bear on them, and through them on the permanent agents of government.

That this is the important question is illustrated by Leslie Chapman in his fascinating exposure of the civil service, *Your Disobedient Servant*. In the Southern Region of the Ministry of Public Works and Buildings (later the Property Service Agency, PSA), which he controlled, he had achieved (with the agreement of the unions and all concerned) economies of the order of thirty per cent in annual expenditure without reduction of service, simply by eliminating waste. Had the people known what he was doing there can be little doubt that it would have been their will that he should succeed in his attempt to persuade the other regions of the Department to follow suit. For the economies amounted to such things as that store-houses which were empty or contained only barbed wire should no longer be heated. One technician was awarded £1,000 for a money-saving suggestion. It was 'Nothing very sophisticated. Nothing very revolutionary. The gas cookers in the mess kitchens are in future to be turned off when not in use!' It would save £40,000 a year.

The responsible Labour Minister did know and did order that Chapman's methods should be adopted elsewhere; but his orders were not carried out. Then came the general election of 1970. The people chose a new government and so a new minister. He too quickly became an enthusiastic champion of Chapman's methods; he too ordered that the example should be followed in the rest of the country; and he too was disobeyed. Now we are engaged in another great round of public expenditure cuts, threatening our schools, hospitals, theatres, and much else that we value; but no doubt the barbed wire in the government store-houses will still be kept warm in the winter.

The power of the people to oust the government is, as Popper so rightly says, the most important power and certainly not to be disparaged. But can we not devise something a little less drastic? I want to point to two existing institutions as a model of how, without radical upheaval, or revolution, we might achieve a kind of plastic control of government at all levels by the governed, by this I mean a control that differs from absolute control as a red traffic light differs from a solid road block. But before I give what seem to me to be the right examples I want to touch on two other current suggestions by way of comparison.

A move in a totally wrong direction is the current tendency to set up non-elected bodies over the heads of elected ones. For example a 'working group' chaired by Mr Gordon Oakes, at that time Minister of State at the Department of Education and Science, proposed the establishment of a national body to oversee generally the development of maintained higher education including the allocation of funds for current expenditure. The body would, in the usual way of these things, have 'representatives' from county councils etc.; but it would in effect, as Tyrrell Burgess (1978) pointed out, control the local education authorities and usurp the Secretary of State's authority, while itself being answerable to nobody and quite out of reach of attack by any member of the public who may not like what it decides. Representatives from local authorities all over the country who meet occasionally in such a body are absolutely powerless against the permanent staff, largely because they do not know each other and have no opportunity to organise themselves in unison. What sort of people are they who devise solutions of this sort, solutions, as Burgess put it, in search of a problem, when the crying need is for a strengthening of the almost non-existent control of the electorate over the L.E.A.s and of Parliament over the D.E.S.?

To many people government by referendum seems to be the ultimate in democracy. Let the people decide every major issue. That must be to their advantage. Mrs Thatcher, before she became Prime Minister, toyed with this idea; but it is a bad one for two main reasons. The first is that the questions of government are usually not of the yes-no kind. Capital punishment is a subject, above all others perhaps, which many people think should be decided by referendum. Mr Albert Pierrepoint, the former official executioner, made my point well when he said: 'The trouble with the (death) sentence has always been that nobody wanted it for everybody, but everybody differed about who should get off.' The best solution to a problem is so often of the kind that I have called lying at right-angles to the yes-no axis. Secondly rational decisions can only be taken in the light of the fullest information. It is simply not possible for the whole electorate to be fully informed on any issue. They must delegate their decision-making to representatives who make it their business to be fully informed; but these representatives do need to be controlled, or tamed, as Popper put it.

Local government

In putting forward my positive suggestions I first draw attention to the important differences between the organisation and functioning of local and central government. I shall use as example the district council of which I am myself a member. The council consists of forty-eight elected members who, like M.P.s, are representatives, not delegates. The work of the council is done by a policy committee and seven 'programme' committees, each with its own field of responsibility, e.g. finance, housing, etc. Each programme committee consists of fourteen elected members. Nine, including the chairman and vice-chairman, are members of the majority party. Four are from the minority party and there is one independent, these being the proportions of the parties in the council as a whole. At each meeting of, for example, the housing committee, there are also present round the table a number of the council's permanent professional staff – the officers. The Director of Housing is there and also a senior officer from each of the following departments: Treasurer's, Planning, Architect's, Estates (dealing with property values, sale of property etc.) Engineer's (roads, parking, sewers etc.) and Secretariat (law, precedent, administration etc.). In the Planning Committee, the Chief Planning Officer would be there in person, while the Director of Housing would normally send one of his staff.

Different authorities have different arrangements in respect of the policy committee. In our case it is chaired by the Leader of the Council, i.e. the leader of the majority party; and it consists of the chairmen of all the programme committees together with four representatives of the opposition. In other councils the opposition are not represented on it. It then functions more like the cabinet, and consists of the Leader, Deputy Leader and the chairmen and perhaps vice-chairmen of all the committees also. (There are important advantages from the point of view taken here, of the control of the rulers by the ruled, in the 'anti-cabinet' system we have. The majority party can always get their way; but they are saved from a number of futile confrontations by being acquainted early on with the opposition's point of view; and sometimes they are not too proud to accept it as better than their own.) The programme committees have certain powers delegated to them by the Council. Their decisions on these matters take effect at once. In others, ratification is required by the Council, which functions more like the House of Commons. There, the officers do not take part.

As in central government, the elected members, the amateurs, ultimately decide (with important reservations which I shall mention later) on each issue that comes before them. Only *they* can vote. Arguments both party political and otherwise can be given a full airing. But the advantages compared to the way that central government operates are these:

1. Each elected member acquires a kind of expertise in the fields of the two or three committees on which he serves.
2. Members of all parties, those in opposition as well as those in power, hear at first hand the advice of the professional officers and read their reports. They have opportunities both in committee and outside to question and cross-examine the officers on their advice (or any other relevant matter) as searchingly as they like.
3. There is continuity. If, as a result of an election, the opposition oust the party in power, the proportions on the committees change; but the new chairman of the housing committee, for example, will normally have been an opposition member of the old committee. He will know the ropes. He will be familiar with the powers of the committee and its obligation under the law. He will know the pros and cons of the controversial matters likely to come before the committee; and he will know the worth or otherwise of the officers who will advise him. Also he will have had a chance while in opposition to work out how the philosophy of his party can be best applied in the circumstances prevailing.
4. New chairmen are not hampered by anything remotely comparable with the absurd restriction placed on new ministers in that they are denied access to their predecessors' papers and plans. The effect of this (and probably the purpose) is that each minister begins from scratch, unaided by any progress made by this predecessor, in his efforts to gain control over his civil servants; and he tends to get moved on before he has begun to achieve it. He is denied the means of learning from previous mistakes. 'The rule is applied', Chapman points out, even when, as in his case, 'the different (Conservative) administration were following identical policies and giving identical instructions.' He, as a

civil servant, was not permitted to tell the new Conservative minister that his Labour predecessor had given identical instructions – for the following up of his (Chapman's) successful elimination of waste – and that the instructions had not been carried out.

5 The elected members have real power over the permanent officials, largely because in the committees where the decisions are taken they outnumber them. The new chairman, supported as he is by a majority of the committee, should be able without much difficulty to carry out the changes of policy which he has decided upon. The corresponding impotence, sometimes, of ministers is well documented. I have already mentioned Mr Callaghan's inability to get an obvious reform adopted by his own department, when he was Home Secretary, until a chief official had been moved on. Mrs Barbara Castle described, while out of office, the difficulties of an inexperienced minister, unsupported as she must be by her political colleagues and surrounded by obsequious civil servants, who say 'Yes, Minister' but are none the less determined to carry on as before. She alone, single-handed, had to try to impose her will and make them switch courses, although she herself must have carried the handicap (which she did not mention in her article) of not really knowing whether what she was trying to persuade them to do was practicable. It is well known how, in the first world war, Lloyd George, even when Prime Minister, was unable to get rid of Haig. Very much with this experience in mind, Churchill, at the very beginning of his administration in 1940, made a small change which 'subject to the support of the War Cabinet and the House of Commons' made him undisputed master in his own house. 'The key change on my taking over', he recorded, 'was the supervision and direction of the Chiefs of Staffs Committee by a Minister of Defence with undefined powers. As the Minister of Defence was the Prime Minister, he had all the rights inherent in that office, including very wide powers of selection and removal of all professional and political personages.' The machinery as well as the men are important. In this connection of the control of officials I remind the reader of the example on

page 117 of the civil servants touring the country preaching a doctrine which was contrary to the policy of the government of the day, someting that local officers could never get away with.

Central and local government compared

Thus the position of the new Housing Chairman contrasts very favourably with the position of the corresponding new Housing Minister in a new government. It is clear from his diaries that in his case Richard Crossman knew nothing about the practical problems faced by his department when he took office in 1964, because he had been 'shadowing' education, and nothing about the way the department functioned or the qualities of its staff. Furthermore he was lumbered, as most new ministers are, with election promises made in ignorance of the facts which gradually confronted him in office. His overall ignorance coupled with his need to appear to be pursuing election 'targets' with all vigour prevented him from interfering, as he might otherwise have done, with the accelerating conversion of the major cities into wastelands or oblongs of reinforced concrete, the at-a-stroke, gimmicky, industrialised building solution to 'the housing problem', resorted to by his predecessors, with such appalling aesthetic and social consequences, not to mention expense, for almost every large town in the country.

It is important to emphasise that the inherent continuity of local government, even where there is a change of political control, does not exclude a change of policy. What it does is to make it more likely that such a change will be rational and practicable, and within the bounds of available finance etc. Nottingham's transport policy is a good example of this. The change of control brought about by the municipal election of 1971 resulted in the discontinuation of a multi-million pound urban motorway scheme and its very successful replacement by a system of bus priorities and car control. (Successful, at least until a further change of political control began to undermine its basis.)

Perhaps the most important advantage of the organisation of District Councils is that all members – those in opposition as well as those in the ruling party – are entitled to know what is going on and to see all letters and reports in which they may be interested. This does not prevent individuals from engaging in corrupt practices; but it does effectively prevent the whole council from pursuing a corrupt, illegal, or hypocritical policy. Nothing like the Rhodesian oil sanctions charade could be undertaken by a district council, because the opposition would expose it. Clearly that twelve-year farce would have been prevented had, say, the shadow cabinet been provided with the same information as ministers. Criticism is the key; but it must be informed criticism. Plenty of people criticised many aspects of the sanctions case; but they were all denied the necessary information which would have made their criticism effective.

Why then does not local government work better than it does? I suggest that there are three main reasons. The first is that there is still no proper link of control and information between the electors and the elected councillors. The electors can throw out their councillor at an election but they cannot control him. Councillors can still get away with supporting schemes that are unrealistic, unpopular, and irrelevant to real needs. Especially is this so in the many local councils where one political party has an almost permanent large majority. The second reason is that it is very difficult for the amateur councillors to get alternative professional advice, alternative that is to that of their officers, who like all professionals, are sometimes wrong but unlike other professionals tend not to disagree enough among themselves. They tend to adopt something of a 'party line'.

These two reasons are linked by the great importance of face-saving. Perhaps it is not surprising that the attitude which Popper persuaded Eccles to adopt in regard to his biological theory which looked like becoming untenable (page 21) has not yet become the norm in local (or central) government. If we have proposed a plan, then it must be right; and no second thoughts, new facts, or new attitudes can be admitted without loss of face. And face is the one thing above all others that must be preserved. If only we could be committed to solving problems rather than to particular solutions!

The third reason is the interference by a central government administration which is ignorant of local conditions and tends to oscillate between one policy and priority and another. In the late 1970s governments of both parties have improved in this respect; but here is the experience concerning housing finance of my own council, not so long ago, in eight months of 1975 to 1976. First of all Whitehall assured us that there would continue to be priority for housing and especially for the improvement of old property. We submit our estimate for the amount we intend to spend in the year ahead on improving old property newly acquired or yet to be acquired by the Council: £950,000. Some months later when we have already spent or allocated £300,000 of this sum, we are told that our allocation has been cut to £350,000; and the reason given for the cut is that available funds must be diverted from less essential matters to where the money can do most good. Among such areas are listed the improvement of old property newly acquired – precisely where our £950,000 was going to be spent. After protest, and pointing out the contradiction, we are given an immediate £70,000 with a hint of possibly more to come. After more argument this is raised to give a final figure of £610,000.

No organisation, however potentially efficient, can function under this kind of harassment. Central government abetted by the media, has always cast local government in a light of ridicule. Local councillors are invariably portrayed as self-seeking, self-important, incompetent figures of fun. Although twenty years before, Crossman had had several years experience as a local councillor, when, in 1964 he was appointed Minister of Housing and Local Government, he took so little interest in the second part of his job that in his first diary entry he describes himself just as Minister of Housing. (And his literary executors carried on this disregard for local government by leaving it out of the title of the first volume.) M.P.s have patronised the councils in their constituencies, often without any attempt to find out how they work; and civil servants have usually regarded as a lesser breed of men their counterpart officers in local government. But the latter have, from the point of view of the public, a great advantage. They are comparatively permanent.

Professor David Henderson, in his analysis of the reasons for bad civil service advice, blamed the anonymity of that advice and the continual shifting of civil servants from one department to another. It is always the department's advice. The individual civil servant responsible has most likely moved on elsewhere by the time the consequences are apparent. 'Not only may it not matter much for your career whether or not you were right, but few will ever know.' 'The Unimportance of Being Right' was the title of Henderson's talks. Whether or not a civil servant is often right is not a factor, Henderson found, in the speed of his promotion. Interestingly enough, in this connection, R. V. Jones said (in his *Most Secret War*), apropos of his having offended certain senior officers by his outspoken criticism of them, 'Nevertheless I survived because war is different from peace; in the latter fallacies can be covered up more or less indefinitely and criticism suppressed, but with the swift action of war the truth comes fairly quickly to light.' And then he quoted Churchill's aphorism: 'In war you don't have to be polite, you just have to be right.'

I am not implying that local government is satisfactory, only that the bones of the system are potentially more capable than those of central government of adaptation to one where government by the people for the people can be carried on. Although, as I have said, councillors are fairly well able to control the officers in the sense of ensuring that they carry out decisions taken at meetings, there is a whole range of matters which never get raised in public. The agenda of committees and councils is to a large extent fixed by the officers; and they tend to bring matters on which they want decisions which are often not the matters on which the councillors would like the searchlight turned.

There is also the technique described by Robert Heller (page 3) and its converse – that is, the under-estimating of the costs of schemes the officers favour and the over-estimating of those they do not. Where decisions *are* required by elected members the situation has too often been manipulated in advance so as to reduce the number of options or to reverse the logical order of things. Left to ourselves, we would never have found ourselves having to make the choice which we are asked to make.

As an example, I cite again the Cumberland Road fiasco in Portsmouth. The Housing Committee were required to decide what to do about the houses blighted by the road scheme before the details of that scheme had been fully worked out, before planning permission for it had been applied for, and long before the obligatory public inquiry could be held. So those councillors who are against the road had to choose between demolition of the houses now, to make way for a road that might never be built, or spending money on them now with the prospect that they might have to come down in a year or two for the road.

Councillors, and I imagine ministers, are constantly put like this into the position of the proverbial Irishman who, when asked the way to Dublin, replied that if *he* were going to Dublin he would not start from here.

Elected members are swamped by more reports than they can possibly read. This has the effect of keeping them quiet for fear of being accused of 'not having done their homework' should they raise some matter on which they are imperfectly informed. However, when occasion demands that the mountains of paper be carefully examined it is not at all unusual to find them faulty. Crossman remarked: 'Once a so-called fact gets into the system it's almost impossible to prove that it's wrong or out of date and should be dropped.' In Portsmouth we have one of these 'so-called facts'. It is a statistic that appeared in a housing survey of 1966 that 57 per cent of the total housing stock was then pre-1914. The same figure appeared as the *present* position in a report to the Council in 1977 although, after a decade of redevelopment a 1976 survey had shown the proportion then to be 43 per cent. Was the overlooking of the 1976 survey from the October 1977 report gross carelessness, or was it a subtle means of influencing, even of frightening, councillors in favour of more demolition? And all the time we are being subtly brain-washed into the assumption that if the proportion of old houses *is* high, that is a disadvatage. A lot could be said for the view that we are lucky to have such a lot of Victorian and Edwardian houses.

Residents' Committees

The second institution which I want to propose, as a model for what could be, is something quite new and still evolving. The miseries and failures associated with the total clearance policies of the 1950s and the 1960s led to policies of conservation and refurbishing. Under the Housing Act of 1969, General Improvement Areas (G.I.A.s) have been declared in most old towns. They are areas of (usually) Victorian houses which, fifteen years ago, would have been scheduled without question for demolition. Each G.I.A. normally contains between 500 and 800 houses. It is a predominantly residential area free of plans for major redevelopment – motorways, shopping centres etc. There are two quite separate prongs to the carrying out of the improvement work. The first is the improvement and modernisation of the houses themselves. It is the second prong that concerns me here.

Money is available from central government for what are called environmental improvements for the area. These are such things as planting of trees and shrubs, renewing pavements, provision of playgrounds, community centres etc., removal of 'non-conforming users' which may be factories which cause a nuisance in the area, road closures and other measures to prevent the use of residential roads as 'dodge runs' for through traffic.

Each G.I.A. has a committeee, composed of from one to three volunteers from each street. The committee, having canvassed their own streets and in consultation with the elected ward councillors and appropriate council officers, decide on a plan for these environmental improvements.

Once a year there is a meeting to which all the residents of the area are invited. They may then give their blessing to what their committee has proposed or air their criticisms of it. It is worth noting that at these meetings, the ward councillors of whatever party, are confronted by the public of all parties or none. This is something which does not happen regularly to M.P.s.

In Portsmouth we have evolved rapidly from having the officers putting up a plan to the Residents' Commitee – and meeting there a deal of hostility – to a cooperative system whereby the officers merely indicate what *could* be done and the residents of the area, through this committee of street representatives, really do control what *is* done. This immediately eliminates the main cause of the adoption of silly plans, namely face-saving. Under this sytem there are no faces to be saved. No matter what the officers think should be done, it is not done if it does not please the residents' committee, and on at least one occasion a plan agreed by such a committee has had to be changed when a full meeting of residents refused to endorse it.

That particular plan was a road scheme which had been set about perfectly rationally. Everybody knew what the problem was. It was to divert, as far as possible, on to main roads the traffic dodging through the area, without making it too difficult for residents to use their own cars. From the start it was realised that there was no perfect solution, and that any plan would have snags and might well increase traffic in some of the streets which at the time had little. Repeated meetings over three years of the G.I.A. committees, and occasional meetings of the City Council's Transportation Committee, and of all the residents concerned, resulted in an experimental plan being tried out and then a modification of that plan in an attempt to iron out snags, partly foreseen and partly not. It has been a satisfactory demonstration of Popperian principle in practice, contrasting starkly with the solutioneering of the larger and infinitely more expensive road schemes I have described elsewhere. It has been successful in eliminating the 'dodge-runners', though less successful in fairly distributing the internal traffic that has to go somewhere.

It is not perfect but it has greatly relieved the suffering of those who were previously tormented by traffic. Without any new construction – merely by making some streets one-way and blocking others – we have made the best of what we have.

We have also achieved an atmosphere in which opinions can be changed in the light of knowledge. Because of the high camber of the old streets and the comparatively low damp courses in the houses bordering them, it has been necessary in some cases, when relaying the pavements, to tilt them towards the houses. Residents' representatives have gone into the meetings vowing that they would not have these new-fangled pavements in *their* street. But the City Engineer's representative came prepared with large clear diagrams illustrating his problem and the alternative solutions. Animosity and opposition evaporated. It was agreed that he should proceed as he thought best.

We have achieved with these committees a degree of the plastic control I mentioned at the beginning of this chapter. Public participation in planning has until recently been little more than a bad joke. A *Guardian* cartoon summed it up by 'And now for something entirely different – two years of debate preceded by the decision'. But in our G.I.A.s a tradition has now been established whereby, although the Council retain the power to override the residents' wishes, they will not do so lightly. They need to have compelling reasons (e.g. that what the residents' want is against the law) which will have to be justified to the residents. The necessity for justification in public is the best way there is for ensuring that at least things will not be done for silly or utterly spurious reasons, as so often they have been in the recent past.

These two examples, showing that at local level there are institutions for the control of government by the governed, contrast with the state of affairs at national level.

Tentative suggestions

My own tentative suggestion is that what are needed to

tame the rulers at all levels are layers of overlapping loops of information and control, modelled on what is already in being. Central government would be gradually reshaped in the direction of the present organisation of the district councils (county councils are even less under control than is central government); and the idea of the G.I.A. residents' committees would be extended. The aim is to achieve informed criticism at all levels enabling information to go both ways – from the governed to the government and vice versa, so that each has some measure of control over the other. We then have to establish these important social traditions, where control is only plastic and not rigid, that the *will of the ruled will not be lightly overruled.*

Probably also we need new institutions to cope with certain technical problems whose complexity prevents their adequate scrutiny by the ordinary committee of lay M.P.s, civil servants, or ministers.

One of the greatest unchecked controls seems to be that exercised by the Treasury over other government departments and over the economy as a whole. At present there are at least three, to some extent contradictory, theories as to the proper direction for the British economy. The Treasury view, in line with the I.M.F. is broadly that everything depends on holding down public expenditure. The keynote of the 'Cambridge policy' however is expansion of the economy combined with a fixing of the level of manufactured imports. A third view, is that of Dr Jeremy Bray M.P. who, using the same model of the economy as the Treasury, comes to very different conclusions. His suggested combination of devaluation, substantial tax changes, and *increases* of public expenditure would, he estimates, greatly increase employment and result in a large favourable balance of payments by 1983/4.

The matter is as important as any that ever comes before Parliament yet it is too technical for it. We need a special institution, a kind of economic forum, where the protagonists can criticise each other in front of an informed audience. The steering of the right economic course is of such importance that it must be justified in public so that it can be seen that science rather than orthodoxy or face-saving has prevailed. It needs to be demonstrated to the lay public that due weight has been given to facts, such as unemployment, and not too much to intangible artefacts like monthly trade figures and relative percentage changes in gross national product (G.N.P.). The danger of such semi-myths is illustrated by the publication just before the general election of 1970 of a £31 million trade deficit for May of that year. It was widely believed at the time that this tipped the scales against Labour; and the feeeling that this was an unfair influence was reinforced by the revision of the figures at the end of that year to show a May deficit of only £12 million. The treacherous nature of the myth is emphasised by the twist in the tail: the latest revision of the figures shows a deficit of £36 million for that May! (*New Society*, 3 August 1978, p. 245).

Similarly the Gross National Product (popularly equated with national standard of living) not only ignores, necessarily, the 'black' economy which has been estimated to run into thousands of millions of pounds (and perhaps explains the fact that we do not appear to be as poor in comparison with, say, the French as the experts tell us we are) but does include such things as production of cigarettes and operations for lung cancer. So that a successful anti-smoking campaign would reduce the G.N.P. in two ways.

In the Conservative party power to decide a policy is kept firmly in the hands of the leader and is not devolved, for the very real fear that the 'backwoodsmen', would take over. In the Labour Party power is vested in the annual party conference and, in theory, policy is there decided by the party activists who are not in fact the same as the 'grass roots' in whose name everything is supposed to be done. As is well known, when the party is in power, the conference is in fact unable to control the government. Genuine devolution in either of the two main parties would undoubtedly result in the adoption of 'extremist' policies which would in no way reflect the wishes of the people as a whole. What I have in mind avoids this difficulty. The series of loops that I suggest between people and both local and central government would be on specific practical issues. The planning of the G.I.A.s is one. The running of the local authority schools might be another. The extremist difficulty would be overcome in three ways. 1) As in the G.I.A.s, the statutory authority would not in any way give up its power to override: 2) people of all political persuasions would be entitled to attend, so that extremist elements would to some extent cancel out; and 3) the practical nature of the agenda would attract, more than do meetings of political parties, those who are interested in practical solutions to problems; and such people tend not to be extremists.

Divisions must be recognised, not smothered. There are bound to be differences of outlook and interest between, for example shopfloor workers and managers and directors. What is required is that there shall be communication between them and some measure of plastic control of each over the other. It is no more good putting shopfloor workers on the board than it would be to put ratepayers in the cabinet.

I do not at all mean to imply that disagreements occur only between the rulers and the ruled and do not arise between different groups or individuals among the governed. But my experience is that if public meetings of the kind I advocate are held, either regularly as an institution or even on an ad hoc basis for a particular problem, then there is a good chance of one of these consequences: 1) Agreement is reached when (a) protagonists of the scheme see how damaging their proposals are to other people, or (b) when objectors realise the reverse – namely how vital the proposals are to the proposers and how comparatively trivial are what they had imagined to be the insuperable snags. 2) Disagreement among the people concerned is so obvious and irreconcilable that, by mutual consent, it is left to the Council to decide.

As an example of (2): a public meeting was held in Portsmouth to air the question of whether to convert a shopping street completely to pedestrian use or whether to leave it as it is at present with buses but no other traffic. The Council's officers and the bus men explained the pros and cons and were questioned by the public. It was obvious that those present were more or less evenly divided between the two possible courses of action. In these circumstances the people were content, I think, for the Council to decide. What had been a heated dispute was disarmed when it was generally recognised that there were good arguments on both sides.

Politicians and newspapers tend to exaggerate the divisions among the people or at any rate to assume that they lie along political party lines, rich or poor, employers and employed, 'capitalists' and workers, etc. In real life partisanship is often much more complicated. Nevertheless division along lines is not to be despised. The benefits it confers become obvious when it is lacking. No party took up the cause against either comprehensive redevelopment, urban motorways, or high-rise prefabricated flats. All these disastrous decisions went through on the nod. The great advantage of opposition is that it forces the airing of the issues with the result that the decision, even if not reversed, is greatly modified in the light of criticism. Popper revers to a generally

> overoptimistic expectation concerning the outcome of a discussion; the expectation that every fruitful discussion should lead to a decisive and deserved intellectual victory of the truth, represented by one party, overfalsity, represented by the other. When it is found that this is not what a discussion usually achieves, disappointment turns an overoptimistic expectation into a general pessimism concerning the value of discussions. ('The myth of the framework')

In conclusion, it obviously detracts from the benefits of having elected representative government if the elected representatives find themselves uable to govern. I have quoted Crossman and Chapman on the subject, and there is plenty of other evidence to the effect that this does happen, that ministers are frequently unable to control their officials. I have described the mechanism of local (district) government in order to demonstrate that it is possible to devise institutions that give the elected rulers effective power, while they themselves are to some extent controlled. 'Institutions are like fortresses', wrote Popper. 'They must be well designed *and* properly manned.' We have tended to concentrate on the manning to the exclusion of the designing. The particular suggestions made in this chapter are advanced in the spirit of the 'bold conjecture' which is then open to attempts to refute it.

To sum up then, my suggestion is that we need at all levels to improve our institutions, and where necessary invent new ones, designed to make possible two-way exchange of information and control – between the public and their elected representatives, between councillors and MPs and their permanent officials, and between the various branches of commerce and industry: manual and office workers, management and providers of capital, and the public for whose benefit the enterprises exist. This must be done, not as a sop to tiresome agitators, but in the realisation that at no level is there a monopoly of knowledge. Each level has its own special kind of knowledge which is necessary to the 'wise wielding of power'.

12

The power of wrong ideas

Certain powerful wrong ideas dominate the mistakes and muddles I have touched upon in this book and at the bottom of them lie the fallacy of induction and ignorance of Popper's solution of the resulting problem. Induction is the cardinal wrong idea. The associated errors are of two kinds. The first assume the validity of induction notwithstanding Hume's conclusion to the contrary, and the second kind, while implicitly accepting the irrationality of induction, go on to assume that there *is* no rationality, that 'human nature' is basically irrational.

The first category comprise the planning errors and the aberrations of certain scientists. They demonstrate a false authoritarianism that is derived from induction because it appears to be possible for authority and experts to know what is right, to arrive in private at the truth or the best solution. The second is at the root of the acceptance of such things as contradictions and the attraction of psychoanalytic or pseudo-psychoanalytic notions which do not need to be justified by reason.

In the early eighteenth century, David Hume had shown that generalisation from a limited number of observations or facts could not be justified by reason; it was not logical to assume that what had not been observed would be the same as what had been. In other words (to use Popper's example), no number of sightings of white swans could make it certain that all swans are white. Yet this process of generalisation seemed to be the basis of rational behaviour and especially of science. We observe that the sun rises every morning, so we assume that it will rise tomorrow and the next day. Hence Hume's conclusion seemed to mean that science and human behaviour in general were not and could not be rational.

The difficulty has arisen out of the mistaken quest for positive confirmations. Induction seemed to be a means of ascertaining the truth. When this turned out not to be valid, it became apparent that there was no direct logical path to certainty. The mistaken quest for certainty led to scepticism and a belief in irrationality.

Popper's solution to the problem is simple. It is based on accepting uncertainty. Rationality consists in making the best choice between approximations to the truth, in making judgements precisely analogous to those made by judge and jury, whose verdicts also are uncertain yet rational. We act rationally, not on generalisations from incomplete experience, but on the best-tested theory, the theory that has best stood up to attempts to refute it. It is true that we act on the theory that the sun will rise tomorrow, but this is not because we generalise from our countless past experiences, but because the theory that it will do so is the one for which we have the best reasons. This interpretation is borne out by the fact that if we were to fly in winter to somewhere north of the Arctic circle, we should expect the sun *not* to rise, because the best theory predicts that it will not, although we as individuals may have no previous experience of perpetual night.

The fact of the invalidity of induction and the nature of the solution of the problem together destroy the case for authoritarianism, élitism, and revelation, and make the case for democracy and science.

If induction were a valid means of arriving at the truth, then civil servants, governments, and authorities of all kinds, and experts in general, could be left to arrive at the truth, the best theory, the best policy, the best solution to a problem. But the fact that the best theory or plan is the one that stands up best to criticism, to genuine attempts to refute it, means that experts alone in private (just like judges in private) cannot be relied upon to arrive at the best answer. They *may* do so; but we shall not know that it is the best until it has withstood severe criticism in public. None of us can be expected to criticise with sufficient severity his own scheme. We see the merits of our own ideas better than others do, but we see their snags much less well. The necessary criticism must therefore come from an outside jury – from other scientists perhaps in the case of science, but from the general public in the case of public affairs, because new laws and plans will affect individuals in ways which they alone know, and which cannot be foreseen (for instance the well-planned law courts that caused more cases to be brought to court) (page 35).

This leads to the idea that a theory cannot be proved although it can, in principle, be disproved. Hence nobody can be sure of the success of a plan or the truth of a theory, while the existence of insurmountable snags or contradictions may often make certain its failure or fallaciousness. It emphasises also that criticism is important and not just 'constructive' criticism. Destructive criticism – pointing out the snags, why something will not work – is far more constructive in the long run than suggesting minor amendments to a fundamentally unsound scheme. On the other hand it is only a short step from the *acceptance* of induction to a belief that theories can be validated by finding enough facts that support them – the process that I have nicknamed white-swanning. I have concentrated on two psychological theories which have been accepted on that sort of basis and which have had a profound effect in undermining the tradition of Western culture. An equally potent and equally invalid complex of theories, Marxism, has been exhaustively criticised by Popper himself in the second volume of *The Open Society*. His main accusation against Marx is that he 'misled scores of intelligent people into believing that historical prophecy is the scientific way of approaching social problems. Marx is responsible', he says, 'for the devastating influence of the historicist method of thought within the ranks of those who wish to advance the cause of the open society' (O.S., ii, 82). This accusation is considered but not, in my view, fully understood or satisfactorily answered in Maurice Cornforth's attempted refutation of Popper. All three theories owe their damaging effect to their explaining of everything in terms of material or unconscious processes, thereby discounting consciousness and therefore reason, that 'medium of universal understanding'. The process could be compared with that of explaining the course of a boat in terms only of the tide and currents while neglecting the efforts of the rowers and helmsman. In Popperian terms it is looking only at World 1 and ignoring World 2. The undercutting of consciousness also leaves out of account the effect of what are usually called cultural influences and what Popper has more accurately defined in his concept of World 3. An appropriate analogy here would be the explaining of the behaviour of motor traffic without taking into account the fact that there is a rule of the road to keep to the left (in the U.K.).

The general indifference to the importance of criticism and the almost universal condemnation of destructive criticism has tragic personal effects. Many of the best young people – the most energetic, enthusiastic, altruistic – are attracted and seduced by meretricious theory-systems such as psychoanalysis and Marxism and more recently by the new cults: Scientology, the Moonies etc. Too often their education has failed to impress on them that, as with the accused in court, the other side must be heard – *audi alteram partem*, the cardinal principle of natural justice, a principle that applies to any kind of decision-making. One must know what is to be said against an apparently attractive creed or case.

Inherent in Popper's solution to the induction problem is a lowering of sights from the unattainable ideals of certainty and perfection to a realistic striving for advance and improvement in knowledge and conditions of life. This can give just as much scope for energy, enthusiasm, and altruism. We must aim to reduce unhappiness rather than try to make people happy, to prevent and cure disease rather than strive for perfect health, reduce poverty and injustice rather than try to create heaven on earth. For we can identify and agree on the bad things; we cannot be sure of and certainly cannot agree on the ideal state of society.

I have concerned myself largely with practical plans about physical things like power stations and roads; but thoughtful people are much exercised by, for instance, the alleged decline of Britain; and by this is meant not just our undoubted failure to increase our Gross National Product in line with that of our neighbours, or our loss of empire, but a decline of the 'whole of society'; and they proceed to find remedies. It is here also, I think, that Popper's attitude is applicable. One must first define the problem. Is it just the G.N.P. or is it also that the trains are dirty or that people are increasingly taking to drink? Next, having defined the problem or problems, we must ask if it is likely that the suggested solution will work or at least help. If this process is carried out, part at least of the problem is likely to disappear. When somebody is suffering from, say, tonsillitis, often he will feel that his whole body is deranged, everything is wrong. Yet the killing of the bacteria infecting those two small organs will quickly restore to health the whole being. So with some of the problems of society. Some may turn out to be genuine but the favoured broad solution irrelevant. A direct remedy is likely to be needed, for example, for keeping trains clean, such as paying the cleaners better and supervising them.

I must add the reason why I suspect that those who attempt this mental exercise will find that the problem largely vanishes or fragments. It is because of the immense diversity of our society, which contains members of the Salvation Army as well as those whose lives revolve around some sort of gambling. It contains the unemployable who spend their 'social security' on ginger wine and it contains the man who without any state aid broke two world athletic records in a week. It contains those who care obsessively about their personal appearance, those whose curlers are in place in readiness for some still more important (but unspecified) occasion, even when the queen comes to their street, and those who don't care at all. There are those who compete in the ballroom dancing championships, those who spend every weekend alone on a river bank under a green umbrella fishing, as well as those with ordinary nine-to-five office jobs who watch 'telly' in the evening. The idea of such a society moving as a whole in any direction other than in terms of total material wealth or power over other peoples seems to be without much meaning.

Finally a couple of disclaimers: in case it may seem that the tendency of this book is anti-technological, anti-progressive, I must emphatically state that this is not the case. The attitude adopted here is substantially that of Winston Churchill's famous remark about scientists, that they must always be on tap, never on top. We must use science and technology in order to better the lot of man, but we must never allow technological progress to be an ideal in itself, overruling what is desirable for man's welfare. We (society, that is, as opposed to individuals) must never do things simply because they are technically possible. In particular we must be wary of computer technology – of the kind of practice exemplified on page 101 – where because factors could not be computed they were taken as being irrelevant or of less importance than those that could be. I would add that I think it most desirable that those who *are* on top, the political and social leaders, should not be illiterate in regard to science and mathematics as so many are today.

It might also be charged that in the last chapter I am advocating a mad proliferation of committees to replace individual decision. This again I am utterly opposed to. There is nothing worse than the artistic choice of a committee. Creation springs from individuals. Committees are necessary as checks on individuals, charged with acting on behalf of the public, to ensure that what they do really is in the public interest. Many committees could be disbanded because they are attempting to do what the individual would do better.

* * *

In summary: this book has been concerned with the consequences of the neglect in public affairs of practical philosophy, and with the way in which wrong ideas, especially unquestioned yet mistaken assumptions and attempted solutions to unformulated problems, can lead and have often led to practical mistakes of many kinds, resulting on the one hand in great economic loss and waste and individual misery and on the other in an atmosphere of distrust of all political and intellectual motives, disillusion with democracy, suspicion of the very idea of truth.

Bibliography

ADAMS, John 1976) 'The appraisal of road schemes', privately circulated (London: University College)

ALLEN, G. Freeman (1976) 'How wagonload freight could be revolutionised', *Modern Railways*, April

ASHER, Richard (1975) *Talking Sense* (London: Pitman Medical)

BELSON, William (1978) *Television Violence and the Adolescent Boy* (London: Saxon House)

BENDIXSON, Terence (1974) *Instead of Cars* (London: Temple Smith)

BERNSTEIN, Jeremy (1973) *Einstein* (London: Fontana/Collins)

BRAY, Jeremy (1978) 'The Treasury's black box', *New Statesman*, 14 July

BROADBENT, Geoffrey (1973) *Design in Architecture* (London, New York: John Wiley & Sons)

BUCHANAN, Colin (1963) *Traffic in Towns* (London: H.M.S.O.)
   (1972) *The State of Britain* (London: Faber & Faber)

BURCH, Philip (1975) 'Spontaneous cell mutation theory', *The Times*, 18 August

BURGESS, Tyrrell (1975) 'Why can't children read?' *New Society*, 3 April
   (1978) 'Solutions in search of a problem', *Guardian*, 25 April

BURKITT, Denis (1979) *Don't Forget Fibre in Your Diet* (London: Martin Dunitz)

CALDER, Nigel (1970) *The Mind of Man* (London: B.B.C.)

CASTLE, Barbara (1973) 'Mandarin power', *The Sunday Times*, 10 June

CHAPMAN, Leslie (1979) *Your Disobedient Servant* (Harmondsworth: Penguin Books)

CHOMSKY, Noam (1959) *Language*, Vol. 35, Jan–March

CHURCHILL, Winston S. (1949) 'Their Finest Hour', *The Second World War*, Vol. 2 (London: Cassell)

CLARK, Kenneth (1969) *Civilisation* (London: B.B.C. and John Murray)

CLARKE, Ann M. and A.D.B. (1976) *Early Experience* (London: Open Books)

CLEAVE, T.L. (1974) *The Saccharine Disease* (Bristol: John Wright & Sons)

COHEN, David (1977) *Psychologists on Psychology* (London: Routledge & Kegan Paul)

COHEN, L. Jonathan (1978) 'Is Popper more relevant than Bacon for scientists?', *Times Higher Education Supplement*, 14 July

CORNFORTH, Maurice (1977) *The Open Philosophy and the Open Society*, 2nd revised edn (London: Lawrence & Wishart)

CRAWSHAY-WILLIAMS, R. (1970) *Russell Remembered* (Oxford University Press)

DAVIE, R., BUTLER, N. and GOLDSTEIN, H. (1972) *From Birth to Seven* (London: Longman)

DAWKINS, Richard (1976) *The Selfish Gene* (Oxford University Press)

DOLL, Richard (1967) *The Prevention of Cancer* (The Nuffield Provincial Hospitals Trust)
   (1972) 'Trends in mortality . . . doctors' . . . smoking habits', *J. Roy. Coll. Phycns. Lond.*, Vol. 6, 2 January

ECCLES, J. C. (1974) in *The Philosophy of Karl Popper*, ed. P. A. Schilpp (La Salle, Illinois: Open Court)

(1977) (with POPPER, Karl R.) *The Self and Its Brain* (London: Springer International)

Electricity Council (1975) *Domestic Sector Analysis 1954/5 to 1974/5* (EF 61) (London: Electricity Council)

ELLIOTT, D. (1979) *Energy Options and Employment* (London: North East London Polytechnic)

Energy Research Group (1976) *A Critique of the Electricity Industry*, ERG 013 (Milton Keynes: Open University)

EYSENCK, Hans J. (1960) *Behaviour Therapy and the Neuroses* (London and Oxford: Pergamon Press)

(1979) 'Race, intelligence, and education', *New Scientist*, 15 March

FEYERABEND, Paul (1975) *Against Method: Outline of an Anarchistic Theory of Knowledge* (London: New Left Books)

GORDON, J. E. (1978) *Structures* (Harmondsworth: Penguin Books)

GRANT, John (1977) *The politics of urban transport planning* (London: Earth Resources Research)

GUY, Frank (1977) 'Unclasp Me', privately circulated (Portsmouth: Polytechnic School of Architecture)

HAMER, Mick (1974) *Wheels within Wheels* (London: Friends of the Earth)

HANLON, Joseph (1976) 'British Rail says: Cheaper by road', *New Scientist*, 9 December

HELLER, Robert (1972) *The Naked Manager* (London: Barrie & Jenkins)

HENDERSON, David (1977) 'The unimportance of being right', *The Listener*, 27 October to 24 November

HITCHCOCK, H. R. and JOHNSON, P. (1932) *The International Style: Architecture since 1922* (New York: W. W. Norton)

HULKE, Malcolm (1977) 'Keep MoT off the road', *New Statesman*, 18 November

JACOBS, Jane (1965) *The Death and Life of Great American Cities* (Harmondsworth: Penguin Books)

JONES, Ernest (1964) *The Life and Work of Sigmund Freud* (Harmondsworth: Penguin Books)

JONES, R. V. (1978) *Most Secret War* (London: Hamish Hamilton)

LAIT, June (1978) 'Social work: retreat from reality', *World Medicine*, 11 January

LITTLE, Arthur (1946 *The Nature of Art* (Dublin: Longman)

MAGEE, Bryan (1971) 'Conversation with Karl Popper', in *Modern British Philosophy*, (London: Secker & Warburg)

(1973) *Popper* (London: Fontana/Collins)

MARCUSE, Herbert (1972) *Studies in Critical Philosophy* (London: New Left Books)

MILL, J. S. (1843) *A System of Logic*, VI

MILLER, George (1966) *Psychology – The Science of Mental Life* (Harmondsworth: Penguin Books)

NICOLSON, Max (1967) *The System* (London: Hodder & Stoughton)

ORWELL, George (1953) *England Your England* (London: Secker & Warburg)

POPPER, Karl R. See page vii

ROBERTS J. M. (1976) *The Hutchinson History of the World* (London: Hutchinson)

RUSSELL, Bertrand (1938) *Power* (London: Allen & Unwin)

(1946) *History of Western Philosophy* (London: Allen & Unwin)

(1948) *Human Knowledge: Its Growth and Limits* (London: Allen & Unwin)

RUSSELL, Claire and RUSSELL, W. M. S. (1961) *Human Behaviour* (London: André Deutsch)

SALTER, Andrew (1951) *Conditioned Reflex Therapy* (London: Allen & Unwin)

SKINNER, B. F. (1957) *Verbal Behavior* (New York: Appleton–Century–Crofts)
   (1973) *Beyond Freedom and Dignity* (Harmondsworth: Penguin Books)
SMITH, Peter K. (1978) 'Is play the best way to learn?', *New Society*, 27 July
STONES, Alan (1977) 'Liverpool now', *Built Environment*, March
STOTT, Denis H. (1978) *Helping Children with Reading Difficulties* (London: Ward
   Lock Educational)
TAYLOR, A. J. P. (1974) in *History of World War I* (ed. A. J. P. Taylor) (London:
   Octopus Books)
TAYLOR, John (1971) 'The shadow of the mind', *New Scientist*, 30 September
TAYLOR, Laurie (1977) 'Freud', *New Society*, 8 December
TAYLOR, Nicholas (1973) *The Village in the City* (London: Temple Smith)
TODD, John W. (1977) 'Then and Now', *World Medicine*, 16 November
Transport Policy (1977) *Transport Policy*, Cmnd 6836, (London: H.M.S.O.)
TYME, John (1978) *Motorways versus Democracy* (London: Macmillan)
WADDINGTON, C. H. (1977) *Tools for Thought* (London: Jonathan Cape)
WARD, Colin (1979) 'Making more mean better', *New Society*, 7 June
WELLS, H. G. (1936) *A Short History of the World* (Harmondsworth: Penguin Books)
WILKINSON, Richard (1976) 'Dear David Ennals . . . ', *New Society*, 16 December
WILMOTT, Peter (1977) 'Brief ideas: the gods that failed', *New Society*, 22 September
WOLPE, Joseph (1948) *Psychotherapy by Reflex Inhibition* (California: Stanford University Press)
WOOD, Derek (1975) *Project Cancelled* (London: Macdonald & Jane's)

Index

abstract society 57–8
Adams, Henry 45
Adams, John 123–4, 183
Adler, Alfred 18
aggression 79
altruism 5, 55–6
anorexia nervosa 23
architect-s, -ure 108–9, 119
Asher, Richard 32–3, 37, 183
authoritarianism 34, 177–8
Ayer, Sir Alfred J. 136
Aztecs 14

Bath 110
behaviourism 5, 69
Belson, William 78, 183
Bendixson, Terence 121, 183
Betjeman, Sir John 110
Bevan, Aneurin 143
Binet, Alfred 83
Bradford-Hill, Sir Arthur 143
Bray, Jeremy 172, 183
British Overseas Airways
    Corporation
    (B.O.A.C.) 154–5
British Rail 61
Broadbent, Geoffrey 35, 183
Buchanan, Sir Colin 110, 183
Bugler, Jeremy 109
Burch, P. R. 143–4, 183
Burgess, Tyrrell 128–132, 159–160,
    183

Callaghan, James 22, 117, 163
Canterbury 110
Castle, Barbara 163, 183
Central Electricity Generating
    Board (C.E.G.B.) 102, 150–2

Central Policy Review Staff 49
certainty 138
    quest for 10, 16, 89, 178
Chapman, Leslie 2, 158–9, 162–3,
    175, 183
Chomsky, Noam 86, 183
Christian, -ity 48, 56, 69
Churchill, Winston S. 82, 133,
    155, 167, 182
CLASP 117
Clark, Kenneth (Lord) 15, 183
Clarke, Ann M. and A.D.B. 90,
    183
Cleave, T.L. 142, 183
Cohen, David 75, 92, 183
Cohen, L. Jonathan 8, 183
collectivism 55
combined heat and power,
    C.H.P. 103, 157
Comet airliner 152–3
comprehensive
    education 41, development 107
Compton, Arthur Holly 24
    his problem 24–25, 71
computers 76, 102, 123, 125, 135
Concorde airliner 2, 104
conditioning 69, 85, 91
    operant- 85
consciousness 28
Conservative party 49, 173
conspiracy 10–1, 61, 74
Copernicus, Nicolas 21, 75–6
cost benefit analysis
    (C.O.B.A.) 101, 123–5
councils
    county 40, 159, 172
    district 160–2, 172
criticism 8, 13, 22, 33, 120, 165,
    180

Crossman, Richard 22, 150, 164, 166, 168, 175, 183

Darwin, Charles 8, 75–6
Davie, Ronald 128, 183
Dawkins, Richard 8, 29, 77, 183
demarcation
  of science 18, 20
democracy 52–3, 178
  relation to science 67–8
Descartes, René 24
  his problem 24–5
diagnosis 81, 138
diet 140–2
discretionary powers 64–6
Doll, Sir Richard 143–4, 183
Donne, John 57
Donnison, David 130–2
dyslexia 132

Eccles, Sir John C. 21, 75, 165, 183
Einstein, Albert 16, 18, 83, 89, 133
electricity supply 102–3, 149–52
emotion 8
empiricism 15–6, 34
Energy Research Group (of Open University) 103, 149–50, 184
equalit-y 34
  -arianism 56
essentialism 53
Euclid 29, 41
Eysenck, Hans J. 20, 91–2, 184

face-saving 165, 170, 173
Fairey aircraft 153–4
Feyerabend, Paul 46, 48, 184
fire-precautions 64–5
Ford car workers 49
Freud, Sigmund 5, 18, 74–8, 84

Galileo 21
Galton, Francis 82–3
General Improvement Areas (G.I.As.) 169–71, 173
Germany 94–5
Godber, Sir George 146

government
  local 160–9, 175
    compared with central 164–7, 175
Grant, John 22, 184
gross national product (G.N.P.) 173, 180–1
growth, linear and exponential 98, 149–50
guilt 81–2
Guy, Frank 117–8, 184

Hampshire 36, 40, 96
Healey, Denis 124
Hegel, Georg W.F. 31
Heller, Robert 3, 61, 168, 184
Henderson, David 167, 184
historicism 5, 42–6
holism 5, 35, 42, 101, 107
hospital building costs 2
houses, -ing 107–113
  'life' of 112, 116
  'improvement' of 116
Howard, Ebenezer 115
Hume, David 14–6, 88, 177
Huxley, Thomas H. 24

illusions
  conceptual 17–8, 89, 91
  optical 90
individualism 5, 55–6, 69
induction 4, 14–17, 20, 136, 177–8
  problem of 14, 180
  solution of 16–7, 178
  an illusion 17
  in relation to democracy 67
intellectualism 34
intelligence and I.Q. 20, 82–4
interventionism
  economic 58, 62
  two kinds of 64–6
irrationalism 8, 31, 32

Jacobs, Jane 106, 111, 184
Jaguar cars 147–8
James, Lord, of Rusholme 65
Jeffery, J.W. 151–2
Jenkins, Roy 156

Jones, Jack 49
Jones, R.V. 136–8, 155, 167, 184

Kaiser, (Wilhelm II) 94–6
Kant, Immanuel 34, 56

Labour government 3, 61
    party 49, 61, 173
language 32, 50
    functions of 13
Liverpool 112
Lloyd George, David 163
local government: see
    government, local
Lorenz, Konrad 77

Magee, Bryan 18, 184
Manchester 112
Marcuse, Herbert 46, 184
Marx, Karl 9, 31, 43, 58–62, 75,
    116, 179
    –ism 6, 48, 50, 179
    vulgar 61
Maudling, Reginald 154
Maynard Smith, John 30
medicine 138
    British and American
        approaches to 139–40
meme 77
metrication 38–9
Mill, John Stuart 46, 48, 71–3, 184
monism 27
motorways 11, 41, 105, 121–6,
    164

National Child Development
    Study 130
National Coal Board 151
National Health Service 2, 43
    reorganisation of 40, 146–7
natural justice 180
natural selection 17
Necker cube 90
Newton, Isaac 16, 84, 89
New York 111
Nicolson, Max 119, 184
nominalism 53

Nottingham 117, 164
nuclear, energy 157
    holocaust 26

oil-firing 2, 103
O.P.E.C. 2
Orwell, George 108, 184
overcrowding (and
        reading) 128–132
Oxford 65
    philosophers 7–8

Pavov, Ivan P. 69, 82, 85
Pericles 55
philosophy
    empirical 15–16, Eastern 69,
        formal 9, linguistic 52
    of meaning 50, of science 6
piecemeal social engineering 35
planning 6, 36, 103–6
    'unplanned' 36, 105
    ideas 96
plans, local 97–8, road 40, 49, 96,
        99, 100–1, 121
    structure 96, war 72, 94–5
'plastic' control 53, 149, 171
Plato 27–8, 34, 55, 158
pluralism 27
Popper, Sir Karl R. 6–7
    on: Adler 18, altruism 55–6,
        centralization 37, 104,
        certainty 16, 89,
        competition 74, conspiracy
        10–12, democracy 52–3,
        equality 34, exploitation 59,
        freedom 6, 59, Freud 18,
        happiness 47, individualism
        55–6, induction 16–18,
        institutions 52, 176,
        interventionism (economic)
        62, (two methods) 64–6,
        Marx 18, 58–9, 179,
        Marxism 6, 48, planning 6,
        103–6, prediction 43,
        repetition 86,
        revolutionaries 52–3, sense
        data 89, social science 3, 17,
        43–4, society (open and

closed) 54–5, 179,
    sovereignty 54, the state 63,
    tyranny 52, Utopianism 47
works by, vii
Portsmouth 44, 96, 108–112, 168,
    170, 174
Property Service Agency,
    P.S.A. 158
psychoanalysis 50, 76, 78
psychologism 5, 48, 72–3
psychology 5, 70–3
Pythagoras 74

rationalism 31–34
    pseudo- 34
referenda 160
relativity 19
Rousseau, Jean Jacques 15
Roberts, J.M. 5, 55, 69, 77, 79,
    184
Roehampton 114
Rover cars 148
Russell, Bertrand 15, 17, 32, 60,
    83, 184
Russell, Claire and W.M.S. 70,
    184

Sandys, Duncan 153
Schlieffen's plan 94, 100
science 23, 69, 178
    demarcation of 18–20
    picture of 19
    objectivity of 13, 49–50
SCOLA 118
Shakespeare, William 9
Shaw, Bernard 61, 108
Skinner, B.F. 85–8, 92, 185
smoking 133, 143–4
social science 12, 43–4
social services,
    reorganization of 40

society as a whole,
    concept of 45, 181
sociology 73–4
    of knowledge 5, 49–50
Socrates 31, 35
solutioneering 3, 40, 101, 121,
    146, 170
Stott, Denis H. 83, 132, 184
systems-analysis 119, 135–6

Taylor, A.J.P. 94, 185
Taylor, Laurie 75, 185
Taylor, Nicolas 113, 185
Thatcher, Margaret 160
Thorndike, E.L. 85, 92
trade unions 49
tradition 45–6, 120
trendism 4, 101
tunnel-vision 4, 17, 65, 101
Tyme, John 126, 184

unemployment 11, 173

verification 18
Vickers aircraft 152–5

Waddington, C.H. 134–6, 185
Watson, J.B. 91
Wells, H.G. 27, 185
Western culture 56, 69, 179
Whitehead, Alfred North 27
white-swanning 4, 22, 83, 144,
    179
whole man,
    treatment of 37–8
Wilmott, Peter 2, 4, 185
Wilson, Sir Harold
Winchester 126
Wood, Derek 153–5, 185
Worcester 110
World 1. 25–27, 182, -2. 25–27,
    182, -3. 25–27, 49, 70, 182

W. SUSSEX INSTITUTE
OF
HIGHER EDUCATION
LIBRARY